LOYOLA KIDS

Book of
Everyday
Prayers

Book of Everyday Prayers

Catherine Odell and Margaret Savitskas

LOYOLAPRESS.

CHICAGO

LOYOLAPRESS.

3441 N. ASHLAND AVENUE
CHICAGO, ILLINOIS 60657

Cover design by Think Design Group
Cover illustration by Craig Marckese
Interior design by Herman Adler Design
Interior illustrations © Art Parts

Library of Congress Cataloging-in-Publication Data

Odell, Catherine.
    Loyola kids book of everyday prayers / Catherine Odell and Margaret Savitskas.
      p. cm.
    Summary: Discusses how, when, and why to pray and offers prayers for many different occasions.
    ISBN 0-8294-1509-2
      1. Children—Prayer-books and devotions—English. 2. Catholic Church—Prayer-books and devotions—English. [1. Prayer—Catholic Church. 2. Prayers.] I. Title: Kids book of everyday prayers. II. Savitskas, Margaret. III. Title.

BX2150 .O33 2002
242'.82—dc21
2001050463

Printed in the United States

02 03 04 05 06 07 08 09 Bang 9 8 7 6 5 4 3 2 1

Devote yourselves to prayer, keeping alert in it with thanksgiving.
—Colossians 4:2

Pray every day! Pray when you are in church

and at home, at school and at play. Pray

whether you are happy or sad, worried or glad.

Pray for every reason under the sun to the

God who made that sun—and everything else.

Pray for yourself and for others. Pray with

confidence and with your heart full of thanks

for God's never-ending goodness. God loves

your prayers. God loves you.

Table of Contents

Introduction

Praying

Praying is a lot like dancing.
Everyone can dance.
And everyone can pray.

EVERYONE CAN DANCE

This happens in a lot of houses where a child is growing up. The baby has learned to stand alone. Maybe he still has to hang on to the edge of a chair, but he is up on his feet. Then someone turns on a radio. If the baby likes the beat, he will bend his knees and start bouncing up and down with the music. He will be smiling and having a great time. Someone else will smile too and say, "Look, the baby is dancing!" Is the baby dancing? Yes! Is the baby dancing the way you dance? No, but you're older!

EVERYONE CAN PRAY

That same baby cannot talk yet, except for a few words like *Da-Da* and *ba-ba*. But one day the baby will be sitting in his high chair at the dinner table. His mom and dad and sister and brother will fold their hands and bow their heads to pray before they eat. The baby will put his chubby little hands together too. Maybe he will clap his hands and coo. Is the baby praying? Yes! In the same way the baby learns to talk, he is learning to pray.

YOU CAN DANCE

Can you do the hula dance? the bunny hop? the Macarena? the jitterbug? the salsa? Can you dance Hip-hop?

Do you like to turn on the radio or put on your favorite CD and just move with the music?

Now maybe you are thinking, *Whoa, I can't dance.* Well, maybe you just think you can't because you feel clumsy or you think you don't do it right. But you can. The secret is the music. All you have to do, really, is listen to the music and respond.

YOU CAN PRAY

Just as there are many kinds of dances, there are many kinds of prayers. You can pray alone or with other people. You can pray out loud or quietly or even without words. You can say prayers of sorrow, praise, thanksgiving, asking, or blessing. Just as you can learn different kinds of dances, you can learn different kinds of prayers too.

Sometimes you make up your own dance to go with the music. You can also make up your own prayer. This is praying too. It comes from inside you. You tell God what is in your heart—what you feel, think, need, wish, hope, and believe.

GOD'S LOVE IS THE MUSIC

Music makes dancing easier. And God's love makes praying easier. Praying is listening to God and responding. Praying is like having a good conversation with someone you trust and can be yourself with.

Picture this: It has rained for three days straight and you have been stuck inside. Then, on the fourth day, the sun comes out. You hop on your bike and pedal down the sidewalk. You splash through the puddles. The air is fresh and cool. The birds are singing. Your heart is happy. You know God made this beautiful day. You know God made you. You smile and say, "God, this is great." You are praying. Now, don't stop there. Thank God for the sun, the birds, even the rain (otherwise, no puddles). Thank God for a healthy body that can enjoy a bike ride.

God is always with you, so you can pray at any time. God is everywhere, so you can pray wherever you are. God is always listening. You don't ever have to leave a message at the beep. Whenever you hear or feel the music of God's love, you are ready to pray. God's love is the music; praying is the dance.

GOD INVITES YOU TO PRAY

Of course, God is much more than music. God is three persons—Father, Son, and Holy Spirit. God loves you and wants your love in return. God is always listening to you, and God understands what you are saying. God is always inviting you to pray—to have a conversation—and to build a relationship.

It helps to remember who God is and who you are. God is a loving Father, and you are God's child. God wants to care for you, to teach you, to protect you, to help you grow, to give you wisdom. All of this happens when you pray.

YOU CAN LEARN TO PRAY

Some children take dance lessons. They learn ballet or tap or jazz. They learn new ways to move their bodies. If they practice, they become better dancers.

Some adults take lessons to learn to dance the waltz or the polka. Some people are professional dancers. Dancing is their job. They may dance in musical shows in a theater on Broadway. They work hard to be the best they can be.

Did you know that some grown-ups devote their lives to prayer? Monks and nuns who live in monasteries and convents pray for many hours every day. They try to be the best pray-ers they can be. This is their way of responding to God's love.

Adults who are teachers and truck drivers, moms and dads, doctors and cooks, dog trainers and factory workers, priests and police officers are pray-ers too. They hear the music of God's love in their hearts and in their lives. They talk to God about what is in their hearts and what is going on in their lives.

Remember, you can pray and you can learn to pray better. You can learn new prayers and new ways of praying. If you pray every day, you will become better at praying.

WAYS TO PRAY

Say a prayer. This is like doing a dance you know really well, like the hokey-pokey. You already know some prayers by heart. The words are always with you, and

you can use them whenever you wish to pray. You can also use the words of others to pray. This book is filled with many prayers. Some of these prayers are from the Bible. There are prayers of Jesus, Mary, and friends of Jesus, and there are psalms. A psalm is a kind of song prayer.

Pray in your own words. This is like listening to the music and making up your own dance. You talk to God about what is happening in your life. You tell God what you are thinking and feeling. God knows everything, including what is happening in your life. But God wants to hear you tell it, because that's the way you get to know God. When you get to know God, you grow into the kind of person God created you to be.

Pray silently. This is like dancing without moving your feet. It is praying without using words. We said that everyone can dance. Maybe you thought, *What if someone is in a wheelchair? How could she dance?* She could move her arms and sway with the music, couldn't she? What if a person is paralyzed and can't move at all? He can dance in his imagination. His spirit can dance beautifully.

This is the prayer of silence. Find a quiet place. Close your eyes. Sit very still. Don't move your feet. Don't move your lips. Be very quiet. Listen to the music of God's love in your soul, deep down inside. Let your spirit respond to God.

Pray during a busy day. This is like dancing and exercising all in one. You know what a busy day is like: go to school, have a piano lesson, eat dinner, study for your spelling test, go to bed. At times like that, you can pray and work all at once. Prayer begins whenever you hear the music of God's love. It only takes a second to think of God and to say, "God, I love you." It only takes a second to whisper, "These spelling words are hard. Help me, Holy Spirit."

Pray all day. This is like a dance marathon. It keeps going and going and going. God is everywhere. God is with you in school, at your music lesson, and on the soccer field. When you have the intention of pleasing God and helping others, prayer springs up. All the kind and loving things you do become a prayer. Caring for the world and those in it is praying. You can begin each day by offering your day to God—everything you will think and do and say. This kind of prayer is called a morning offering. You can find several in this book, or you can use your own words.

Pray while walking. This is like slow dancing. Find a partner— maybe your mom or dad or a grandparent. Take a short walk around your neighborhood, on the beach, or in the park. Pay attention to God's beautiful creation. Thank God for what you see and hear. Talk with your walking partner about the good things and the bad things in your life. Together, ask God to take care of everything.

Pray with others. This is when everyone gets out on the dance floor! Jesus said, "If two of you agree on earth about anything you ask, it will be done for you by my Father in heaven. For where two or three are gathered in my name, I am there among them" (Matthew 18:19–20). You gather with others in Jesus' name when you pray with your class, with your family, and with your parish.

MANY VOICES

When you go to Mass on Sunday your voice is one of many voices joined in song and prayer. Even when you are alone, you can pray with Jesus, Mary, saints, and angels. Everyone who loves God is united in God's love. That is why you will find many voices in this book—the voices of Jesus, Mary, the saints, and other children. That is why you can ask the angels and saints to pray for you and with you. In heaven and on earth, at every moment, many voices praise God. Join in!

KINDS OF PRAYER

- **Prayer of praise**—when you say how great God is.
- **Prayer of thanksgiving**—when you say thank you for God's gifts.

- **Prayer of asking**—when you ask for God's help.
- **Prayer of sorrow**—when you tell God you are sorry for your sins and ask for God's forgiveness.
- **Prayer of blessing**—when you ask for God's blessing for yourself or other people.
- **Prayer of action**—when you pray with your body. Genuflecting, kneeling, and standing are action prayers you do at Mass. Bowing, folding your hands, and making the sign of the cross are other action prayers.

TIMES TO PRAY

There are many times when you can pray. In this book, you will find prayers for all of these times.

In church. One of the most important times when we pray is at Mass on Sundays. Every week the Catholic community gathers together to worship God. In the Mass there are prayers of thanksgiving, prayers of sorrow, prayers of praise, prayers of asking, and prayers of blessing. There are many action prayers too, such as singing in church. After Communion is a special time for you to pray to God

on your own. At that time you can also visit Jesus, who is present in the Blessed Sacrament.

During the day. You can form a good habit of praying at certain times during the day: in the morning and at bedtime, at meals, when you go out, before a class or game, and before you study.

On special days or at special times of the year. Special days like birthdays, Christmas, Valentine's Day, and the first day of school deserve special prayers.

When others need God's help. You can pray for your family, friends, teachers, someone who is sick, or people who have been hurt.

When you are happy, sad, or worried. You can pray no matter how you are feeling. God cares and understands.

Chapter 1
Prayers When I'm Happy

You Make Me Happy

Dear God,

I just feel good knowing that you love everyone everywhere. That makes me happy.

Rhonda, age 9

PRAYERS FOR CREATION

God Made the World!

God made the world, so broad and grand,
Filled with blessings from his hand.
He made the sky so high and blue,
And all the little children too.

Anonymous

 DID YOU KNOW A canticle is a poem or prayer that is easy to sing. St. Francis was once a wealthy nobleman and knight. In his day, knights often wrote canticles praising beautiful ladies. Later, Francis wrote canticles praising God's beautiful creation.

Canticle of the Sun

Be praised, my Lord,
For all your creatures,
And first for brother sun,
Who makes the day bright and luminous.

He is beautiful and radiant
With great splendor.
He is the image of You,
Most high.

Be praised, my Lord,
For sister moon and the stars.
You placed them in the sky,
So bright and twinkling.

Be praised, my Lord,
For brother wind,
For the air and the clouds
And the airy skies
And every kind of weather,
Through which you give
Nourishment to all your creatures.

Be praised, my Lord,
For sister water,
Who is very useful
And humble and precious and pure.

Be praised, my Lord,
For brother fire,
Who illuminates the night.
He is beautiful and joyous,
Robust and strong.

Be praised, my Lord,
For our sister, mother earth,
Who keeps us and watches us
And brings fruit and grain

Of all kinds,

Multicolored flowers

And herbs.

St. Francis of Assisi (1181–1226)

A World of Thanks

God, creator of the universe,

thank you for the stars and the moon,

the sun and the planets.

Thank you for birds and animals,

trees and people.

Thank you for your love and care.

Help us to take care of the earth.

Jonathon, age 8

 Five hundred years before Jesus lived, Babylonia conquered the Jews. When three young Jews, friends of Daniel, refused to worship a gold statue, they were thrown into a blazing furnace. God's angel saved them! They sang this beautiful song of praise to God.

Song of Praise

All things bless the Lord who created them.

Listen to nature's wordless song of praise!

Bless the Lord, sun and moon;

Bless the Lord, stars of heaven;

Bless the Lord, all rain and dew;

Bless the Lord, all you winds;

Bless the Lord, fire and heat;

Bless the Lord, winter cold and summer heat;

Bless the Lord, dews and falling snow;

Bless the Lord, ice and cold;

Bless the Lord, nights and days;

Bless the Lord, lightnings and clouds.

Let all things on earth and in water also bless the Lord.

Bless the Lord, mountains and hills;

Bless the Lord, all that grows in the ground;

Bless the Lord, you springs;

Bless the Lord, seas and rivers;

Bless the Lord, you whales and all that swim in the waters;

Bless the Lord, you birds of the air;

Bless the Lord, all wild animals and cattle;

Bless the Lord, all people on earth.

Daniel 3:62–82, adapted

DID YOU KNOW   In Genesis, the first book of the Bible, in chapters 1 and 2, you can read the story of creation.

Song of Creation

Long, long ago you said, "Let there be light."

In a moment or two, you made day and night.

Then came the water and just enough land.

The world as we know it was shaped by your hand.

Then vegetables, fruit trees, cacti, and flowers

Grew out of nothing, displaying your powers.

The world was so beautiful, shining and new.

The valleys were green; the skies were bright blue.

Then lions and lizards, chipmunks and deer,

Blue jays and dolphins you gave to us here.

With growling and buzzing, with chirping and squawking,

Your new creatures filled the whole earth with their talking.

You listened and laughed at this noisy earth song.

It wasn't quite right, though it wasn't all wrong.

Some speech from our planet was missing, you knew.

So you fashioned new creatures in the image of You.

A man and a woman, the first of our race,

Began to draw breath in the garden of grace.

You said it was good and delightful to see.

Earth was alive; life was precious and free.

Thank you, Creator, for all that you've done.

With love we've been fashioned and cared for and won.

Catherine Odell

All Things Bright and Beautiful

All things bright and beautiful,

All creatures great and small,

All things wise and wonderful,

The Lord God made them all.

Each little flower that opens,

Each little bird that sings,

He made their glowing colors,

He made their tiny wings.

The purple-headed mountains,

The river running by,

The sunset and the morning,

That brightens up the sky.

The cold wind in the winter,

The pleasant summer sun,

The ripe fruits in the garden,

He made them every one.

He gave us eyes to see them,

And lips that we might tell,

How great is God Almighty,

Who has made all things well.

Cecil Frances Alexander (1818–95)

I Like Insects, God

I like insects, God.

I have boxes for snails, and jars for spiders and ladybugs.

I found spider eggs and put them in bottles.

I also caught one worm and two little furry worms.

When you touch them, your hand starts to itch.

All the insects are in my room.

I still want to catch a small lizard, a tadpole, some fireflies,
    and a snake . . .

Dear Jesus, I want you to bless the insects so that people
    won't kill them.

And when I am big, I want to be a vet or
a scientist.

Amen.

Leshan, age 8, Sri Lanka

PRAYERS THAT PRAISE GOD

At All Times

I will bless the Lord at all times;

His praise shall be continually in my mouth.

Glorify the Lord with me,

Let's together glorify his name.

Psalm 34:1–3, adapted

Rejoicing at Dawn

Sing praises to the LORD, O you his faithful ones,

and give thanks to his holy name.

For his anger is but for a moment;

his favor is for a lifetime.

Weeping may linger for the night,

but joy comes with the morning.

Psalm 30:4–5

Make a Joyful Noise

Make a joyful noise to the LORD, all the earth.
  Worship the LORD with gladness;
  come into his presence with singing.

Know that the LORD is God.
  It is he that made us, and we are his;
  we are his people, and the sheep of his pasture.

Enter his gates with thanksgiving,
  and his courts with praise.
  Give thanks to him, bless his name.

For the LORD is good;
  his steadfast love endures forever,
  and his faithfulness to all generations.

Psalm 100

The Way I'm Made

I have two eyes that wink and blink.

I have a mind to make me think.

I have two hands that clap for fun.

I have two feet that jump and run.

I have two ears to hear a song.

I have a body, sure and strong,

Two lips to praise God all day long.

Anonymous

Praised Be God

Praised be

my Lord God

for all his creatures.

St. Francis of Assisi (1181–1226)

I Sing for Joy

God, your never-ending love is better than life!

My lips will always praise you.

And I will bless you as long as I live;

I will lift up my hands and pray to you.

My spirit is fed as with a rich feast.

And my mouth praises you with joyful lips.

Psalm 63:3–5, adapted

Sing to the Lord!

O sing to the LORD a new song;

    sing to the LORD, all the earth.

Sing to the LORD, bless his name;

    tell of his salvation from day to day.

Declare his glory among the nations,

    his marvelous works among all the peoples.

Psalm 96:1–3

Did you Know

When Mary visited her cousin Elizabeth, Elizabeth's unborn baby, John, jumped for joy in her womb. Elizabeth knew that Mary was the Savior's mother. Mary was so happy! She had to praise and thank God.

Mary's Happy Song

My soul proclaims the greatness of the Lord.
My spirit rejoices in God, my Savior,
For he has looked upon my lowliness.
Behold, from now on, all ages will call me blessed.
God, the one who can do all things,
Has done great things for me.
Holy is his name!

Luke 1:46–49, adapted

Clothed with Glory

Bless the LORD, O my soul.
　O LORD my God, you are very great.
You are clothed with honor and majesty,
　wrapped in light as with a garment.
You stretch out the heavens like a tent,
　you set the beams of Your chambers on the waters,
you make the clouds your chariot,
　you ride on the wings of the wind,
you make the winds your messengers,
　fire and flame your ministers.

Psalm 104:1–4

When St. Faustina was growing up in Poland, her family was very poor. She even had to share a dress with her sisters. But she felt that she had everything she needed. From an early age, she understood that God's love and mercy are unending. She spent her life telling others about God's mercy.

God's Mercy Is Reason for Joy!

Praise God for everything and give him glory.

His goodness and mercy are endless.

God, even in the hard and sad times, I see your great mercy.

By disciplining us now, you free us from eternal punishment.

Rejoice! All of us are closer to God's merciful heart than
a baby is to the mother's heart.

O God, you have such compassion for sinners who are
really sorry.

The greatest sinner has the greatest claim on your mercy.

St. Faustina Kowalska (1905–38),
adapted

PRAYERS THAT THANK GOD

 St. Catherine and her twin were the youngest in a family of twenty-five children. She loved God deeply and understood how deeply God loves all people. She served the sick and poor in Siena, Italy, and wrote about God's love.

A Saint's Thank-You

O tender Father,
You gave me more, much more
Than I ever thought to ask for.

I see that what I want
Is such a tiny part of
What you want to give me.

Thanks,
And again thanks, O Father,
For having granted my request.
Amen.

St. Catherine of Siena
(1347–80), adapted

Thanks for My Baby Sister, God

Thank you, God, for this new and wonderful baby sister.

She is the sun behind me.

God, you are the moon in front of me.

I love my new baby sister.

Daniel, age 8

God Bless Our Baby

God bless the baby's beautiful little heart. The baby will be good and loving. Baby fingers are small and long like baby carrots. Someday, the baby will be kind and helpful. The new baby gets lots of attention. But there is still some for me. Soon, the baby will be talking and walking. I pray to God to help me not to do bad things, for the baby is watching and does what I do. I will not be jealous. Instead, I'll be happy. Thank you for making me a new baby sister.

Amanda, age 10

Thanks for Heaven

Dear God,

Thank you for having a wonderful place where we go
   when we die.

Open the gates of heaven.

Proclaim your joyous words.

Keep us together forever. Amen.

Danielle, age 10

You Watch over Us

Dear God,

Father of us all,

Thank you for all the blessings that you give us.

Thank you for watching over us and protecting us
   every day.

I thank you in Jesus' name. Amen.

Chelsey, age 10

Prayer of Jesus

Father, I thank you for having heard me.

I knew that you always hear me.

John 11:41–42

PRAYERS FOR GOD'S HELP

Come, Holy Spirit

Come, Holy Spirit.

Come, Holy Spirit, into my life.

Help me with the good times and the bad times.

Come, Holy Spirit, into my life.

Help me to be happy when I lose a game, or when I win.

Come, Holy Spirit, into my life.

Erica, age 9

Be with Me, God

God, be with me in my heart as I pray.

Thank you for my pets, food, family,

home, and grandma and grandpa.

I will always love you and never stop loving you.

Amanda, age 8

Lord, Help Me

Lord, help me
to find the good . . .
and praise it!

Anonymous

A Little Light

God
Make my life
A little light
Within the world
To glow;
A little flame
To burn bright,
Wherever
I may
Go.

Traditional prayer from England

A Clear Day

Dear Lord on high,
Make a clear sky,
Make the day fine,
And let the sweet sun shine.

Traditional prayer from Holland

Children of the Light

Live as children of the light,
for light produces every kind of goodness and truth.
For all you are children of the light
and children of the day.

Ephesians 5:8–9 and 1 Thessalonians
5:5, adapted

Summer Vacation Prayer

No more homework, no more tests.
No more getting up for school.
No more book reports or studying.
My summer vacation begins today!
I'm so happy and I'm so free.
I want to read and get up late.
I want to ride my bike and swim.
I want to play more with my friends.
Please bless my summer days, dear God.
Keep me safe and happy.

Catherine Odell

PRAYERS OF LOVE

So Much Love

God, I love you so much that
I can't love anybody more than you.

Nikolas, age 6

All about God

God is. I know that.
God made me—I'm glad he did.
God loves me—I need to know that.
I believe in God.

Child's prayer from New Zealand

The One Who Prays

The one who prays best is the one who loves best
All things both great and small;
For the dear God who loves us,
He made and loves us all.

Samuel Taylor Coleridge (1772–1834),
adapted

You Are Always with Me

Dear God,

When I pray, you make me really happy.

I like to pray to you, God.

Everywhere I go, I know you are always there with me.

Caitlin, age 7

One Little Heart

Two little eyes to look to God.

Two little ears to hear his word.

Two little feet to walk his ways.

Two little lips to sing his praise.

Two little hands to do his will,

And one little heart to love him still.

Traditional prayer from Wales

Happy Is the Child

Happy,

Happy is the child.

Happy is the child in a home full of love.

Happy is the child in a home full of love in a city of faith.

Happy is the child in a home full of love in
a city of faith in a nation at peace.

Happy is the child in a home full of love in a city of faith in
a nation of peace in an understanding world.

Happy is the child in a home full of love in a city of faith in
a nation at peace in an understanding world
beneath the warm wings of God.

Happy is the child.

So very happy.

Catherine Odell

Chapter 2
Prayers When I'm Sad

A Cry for Help

Listen, O Lord, to my prayer;
   hear my cry for help.
In the day of my trouble I call on you,
   for you will answer me.
For you, O Lord, are good and forgiving,
   always full of love to all who call on you.

Psalm 86:5–7, adapted

PRAYERS FOR GOD'S MERCY

I Am Lonely and Sad

To you, O LORD, I lift up my soul.

O my God, in you I trust; . . .

Turn to me and be gracious to me,

   for I am lonely and afflicted.

Relieve the troubles of my heart,

   and bring me out of my distress. . . .

   Forgive all my sins.

Psalm 25:1–2, 16–18

Be Merciful

Be merciful to me, O God, be merciful to me,

   for in you my soul takes refuge;

in the shadow of your wings I will take refuge,

   until the destroying storms pass by.

Psalm 57:1

Waiting for God's Help

Out of the depths I cry to you, O Lord.

   Lord, hear my voice!

Let your ears listen

   to the sound of my cry!

I wait for the Lord, my soul waits,

   and in his word I hope;

my soul waits for the Lord,

   more than those who watch for the morning.

Psalm 130:1–2, 5–6, adapted

 DID YOU KNOW Children in Ecuador say this prayer much as children in the United States say, "Rain, rain, go away . . ." But you can say this prayer when sad tears are falling and you want to see God's sun shining in your life again.

Prayer for the Rain to Stop

Farmer St. Isidore,

Take away the rain

And bring the sun out

Once again.

*Traditional prayer
from Ecuador*

St. Peter said this prayer while he was walking on the water toward Jesus. He became very afraid and called out to Jesus. His prayer is very short. You can use it any time you are in trouble.

Prayer of St. Peter

Lord, save me!

Matthew 14:30

You can repeat this prayer until you feel the peace and comfort of Jesus. Or you can simply pray the name "Jesus" in your heart, over and over.

The Jesus Prayer

Lord Jesus Christ, Son of God,
have mercy on me, a sinner.

Traditional

DID YOU KNOW

You can read the story of the lost sheep in Luke 15:3–7.

Lord, Have Mercy

Show me, O Lord, your mercy. I am the sheep who wandered into the wilderness—seek after me, and bring me home again to your fold.

St. Jerome (c. 340–c. 420)

Holy Spirit, Be with Me

Holy Spirit, be with me now. Be in my heart always. Help me when I need help the most. Amen.

Meghan, age 8

Help Me Through

O my God, help me through my hard times when I need you. Help me do what's right and ignore temptation.

Sofia, age 9

On the night before he died on the cross, Jesus prayed in the Garden of Gethsemane. He was afraid of what was to come. Out of love, Jesus told his Father that he would accept this suffering. He knew that his death was part of God's plan to save us from sin and eternal death.

Jesus Speaks about His Death

Now my soul is troubled. And what should I say—
"Father, save me from this hour"? No, it is for this reason
that I have come to this hour. Father, glorify your name.

John 12:27–28

St. Jude was one of Jesus' apostles. He is the patron saint of impossible cases. But St. Jude knows that nothing is impossible with God. Ask St. Jude to help you pray when you need God's help the most.

Prayer to St. Jude

Holy St. Jude, friend of Jesus, help me today. I need God's
help to _____. Holy St. Jude, pray for me.

Margaret Savitskas

DID YOU KNOW The soldiers made fun of Jesus before he died on the cross. They dressed him like a king with a crown of thorns. They slapped him and spit on him and laughed at him. Jesus knows how it feels when someone makes fun of you. You can always ask Jesus for help.

When Feelings Are Hurt

Dear Jesus, my heart is hurting. A kid at school said something mean about me. The other kids laughed. I thought they were my friends! They made me sad and angry. I wanted to cry. I wanted to scream at them. Please help me to be strong. Please help me to forgive.

Arturo, age 12

Mom Yelled at Me

My mom yelled at me. I know I goofed up—again! But I hate it when she yells. It hurts. Help me to think before I do the wrong thing. And please help my mom to be calm. I will tell her I'm sorry. Please help me, Lord.

Ben, age 11

When Parents Fight

My parents aren't getting along. When they fight I feel bad. Why can't they just be friends? That's what they say to me and my sister. So I know it's not always so easy. I love my mom and I love my dad. I know they love me, too. God, help them to love each other. Or at least to be friends. Amen.

Audra, age 11

Missing Dad

I miss my dad. He says he misses me, too. I wish he could come home. Please watch over him when he is gone. Help him when he is feeling alone. Maybe he will call me today.

Quincy, age 10

Losing a Game

Jesus, we lost the game. I really, really wanted to win this one. I feel like blaming some people on the team. Please help me to be kind and not to think I am better than they are. Help me to remember that we need everyone on the team. I hope we can win next time. I will do my best. And I will try to help everyone do their best, too.

Allison, age 12

St. Francis of Assisi loved all of God's creatures. It is said that he talked to the birds about God's love for them—and they listened!

When a Pet Dies

Gentle St. Francis,

I love my pet, _____. You know how I feel because you love animals, too. My pet died. I am so sad. I miss my pet very much. Please watch over my pet in heaven. May God bless and take care of all animals. Amen.

Margaret Savitskas

PRAYERS FOR GOD'S COMFORT

This is a song of David, the shepherd boy who became king of Israel. He also killed the giant Goliath.

The Lord Is My Shepherd

The LORD is my shepherd, I shall not want.
　He makes me lie down in green pastures;
he leads me beside still waters;
　he restores my soul.
He leads me in right paths
　for his name's sake.

Even though I walk through the darkest valley,
　I fear no evil;
for you are with me;
　your rod and your staff—
　they comfort me.

You prepare a table before me
  in the presence of my enemies;
you anoint my head with oil;
my cup overflows.
Surely goodness and mercy shall follow me
  all the days of my life,
and I shall dwell in the house of the LORD
  my whole life long.

Psalm 23

When I Am in a Dark Valley

God, no valley is too dark if you are with me.
I would rather walk in deep mountain shadows with you
    than on a bright sunny beach without you.
God, don't let go of my hand—not even for a minute. I
    need you. I will hang on tight to you. Amen.

Margaret Savitskas

Show Us the Way

Lord of Love,
When we are feeling down, you comfort us.
When we are sad, you make us happy.
When we take the wrong path, you show us the right
    way to heaven, your home.

Fredericka, age 10

When I'm Sad

Dear God, when I'm sad I like to think about all the beautiful things you created. Thank you for the animals and plants. Thank you for making all the beautiful things in the world. Thank you for letting your Son, Jesus, die for us so that we may be happy in heaven with you. Amen.

Joseph, age 10

In the Dark Times

As the rain hides the stars,

as the clouds hide the blue of the sky,

so the dark times of my life

hide the shining of your face from me.

Yet, if I may hold your hand in the darkness,

it is enough.

Because I know that, though I may stumble in my going,

you do not fall.

Traditional Gaelic prayer

God, I Need Help!

O Lord, please hear my prayer
   and my cry for help.
Do not hide your face from me
   in the day of my distress.
Turn your ear toward my cry;
   answer me quickly when I call.
My days vanish like smoke,
   and I wither away like the grass.

Psalm 102:1–4, adapted

My Friend Is Moving

God, I am sad because my friend is moving away. I'm afraid I won't ever be happy again. I need comfort on that day. So could you be at my side on the very last day?

Kathryn, age 10

I Am Moving

God, please help me with the move, so far away from here. Help me make some new friends that are just like the old. Help me to get adjusted and to have fun again. Please, be with me.

Kyle, age 10

A New Baby? I Don't Know . . .

Mom smiled a lot and said:

"We're going to have a new baby!"

I'm sure you already knew, God.

Dad says, "Babies are blessings from heaven!"

I was surprised by this news.

I was sad and scared too.

Help me, God, to be happy.

Bless my mom and the new baby coming to our house.

Help me to smile like Mom smiles.

Catherine Odell

St. Thomas Aquinas (c. 1225–74) was born in Sicily. He loved God and learning. He was big—6'5"—but also shy. Students called him "the dumb ox." Actually, Thomas was brilliant. He became a Dominican priest and teacher. He is the patron saint of Catholic schools and of all students.

St. Thomas Aquinas, Are You Good at Math?

Dear St. Thomas Aquinas,

I cried when I got my math test back today.

I got a bad grade . . . and I studied hard!

I want to learn. I want to get good grades and understand my math problems.

But I need your help.

Please ask the Lord to help me to learn.

Help me to keep on trying and to ask my teacher the right questions when I don't understand.

I'm counting on you . . .

Do you get it?

I know that you loved the Lord

And I know that you counted on him.

Catherine Odell

PRAYERS FOR GOD'S FORGIVENESS

When I Stumble

Lord, I am sorry for offending you. You are my God and I am your servant. I will do my best to follow you. When I stumble, pull me back, please. Help me, God.

Peter, age 10

Lord, Forgive Me

Jesus, I kneel at your feet. You give so much, yet expect so little. I am sorry for the times when I don't even give that little bit. I am sorry for the times I sin and for the times my brothers and sisters sin. Lord, please forgive me. Amen.

Katelyn, age 10

When I Have Done Wrong

Dear God,

I am really, really sad. I did something wrong. I know I
hurt other people, and I hurt you, too.

You know what I did, don't you, God? I am very sorry.

You still love me, don't you, God? Please forgive me.

Help me to tell the truth about what I did. Help me, please.

Antonio, age 11

DID YOU KNOW   St. Monica sent her son, Augustine, to religion classes. Young
Augustine was very intelligent, but he put off being baptized because he was not
ready to be good. Augustine looked for happiness in the pleasures of this world.
His mother prayed for him all this time. Finally, Augustine discovered that it was
God he was looking for. Then he became a priest, a bishop, a great writer, and
a saint.

A Restless Heart

O God, you have made us for yourself, and our heart is
restless until it rests in you.

St. Augustine (354–430)

PRAYERS FOR PEACE

Make Me Holy

Come, Holy Spirit,
   give me wisdom.
Come, Holy Spirit,
   give me joy.
Come, Holy Spirit,
   give me patience.
Come, Holy Spirit,
   give me peace.
Come, Holy Spirit,
   make me loving.
Come, Holy Spirit,
   make me pure.
Come, Holy Spirit,
   make me strong.
Come, Holy Spirit,
   make me kind.
Come, Holy Spirit,
   make me holy.

Margaret Savitskas

Did you know Clement was the third pope after St. Peter.

Children of Peace

O God, make us children of quietness
and heirs of peace.

St. Clement of Rome (died c. 101)

Prayer for Peace

Lead me from death to life,

from falsehood to truth.

Lead me from despair to hope,

from fear to trust.

Lead me from hate to love,

from war to peace.

Let peace fill my heart, my world, my universe.

Amen.

Pax Christi

For Peace in the World

Lord our Father, bring peace to people in our country
and in the rest of the world.

Help those who are homeless and those who do not have
something to eat.

Bring peace in the whole world. Stop all the wars in
countries and give people the peace they need. Amen.

Clare, age 10, Uganda

Chapter 3

Prayers When I'm Worried

Dear God, Be Good to Me

Dear God, be good to me,
The sea is so wide and my boat is so small.

Prayer of the Breton fishermen

PRAYERS FOR RELIEF

A Prayer for Peace in My Country

Dear Jesus,

I pray for our soldiers going to war, and I pray that we
will soon have peace talks.

I wish we could have peace with the next-door neighbors.

Now, they throw bombs or send missiles.

I can never go near some places because someone sends
those bombs there.

I wish there could be peace and harmony.

Then I could go out and see other places in my country.

Then I would help soldiers and people who have lots
of wounds,

and I would also help the widows.

Romal, age 10, Sri Lanka

DID YOU KNOW Once, a Canaanite woman asked Jesus to help her daughter, who was tormented by a demon. The woman was not a Jew, and Jews were not supposed to even talk to non-Jews. But Jesus heard her prayer and cured her daughter. You can read this story in Matthew 15:21–28.

The Shortest Prayer in the Bible

Lord, help me.

Matthew 15:25

Hurry, God!

Agree, O God, to rescue me;
   Lord, hurry to help me!

Psalm 70:1, adapted

Bedtime Stomachache

God, my stomach hurts.
Mom gave me medicine that was supposed to help.
But it didn't.
So Mom hugged me and sat on my bed for a long time.
I could tell that she was worried.
She said what she usually says:
"Let's see how you are tomorrow morning."
Tomorrow morning is pretty far away, God.
Can you help me tonight?

Catherine Odell

DID YOU KNOW Bernadette was fourteen years old when the Blessed Virgin appeared to her in a rocky cave in France. Many people doubted Bernadette's story. She was poor and could not read. Later, as a nun, she suffered and died from tuberculosis. Some people said that she pretended to be sick to avoid work. Bernadette ignored their mean words, thinking of the beautiful Virgin and of Mary's Son, Jesus.

Your Cross and My Cross

O Jesus! Jesus!

No longer do I feel my cross when now I think of yours!

St. Bernadette of Lourdes (1844–79)

Prayer for Parents Who Argue

Jesus, I don't think my parents are very happy together.

They argue too much.

My mom cries and throws her clothes in a heap.

Daddy leaves the house or turns on the ball game
    really loud.

I don't know why they argue about money or whose job
    it is to put gas in the car.

Maybe they are really unhappy
    about something else.

I don't understand, but it scares me
    and makes me sad.

In the Gospel, Jesus, I read that you multiplied the five
    loaves and two fish.

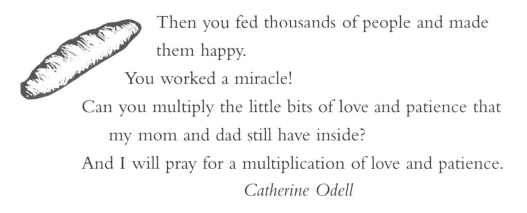

Then you fed thousands of people and made them happy.

You worked a miracle!

Can you multiply the little bits of love and patience that my mom and dad still have inside?

And I will pray for a multiplication of love and patience.

Catherine Odell

DID YOU KNOW The angel Gabriel visited Mary and asked her to be the mother of Jesus, the Son of God. You can read the story in Luke 1:26–38.

When I'm Afraid

"Don't be afraid."

That's what the angel said to Mary.

"Don't be afraid. God loves you."

God, I am afraid.

I am afraid of what you want me to do.

I'm afraid that someone will make fun of me.

I'm afraid that I can't do it.

Please send an angel to whisper in my heart,

"Don't be afraid. God loves you."

I will be listening, God.

Margaret Savitskas

St. Anthony of Padua (c. 1191–1231) was a Franciscan at the time of St. Francis of Assisi. Anthony's talks about Jesus were so wonderful that crowds followed him. Some said that even the fish lifted their heads out of the water to hear him as he talked near the shore. Once, Anthony lost his prayer book. He prayed and prayed until it was returned by the monk who had stolen it.

Oops, St. Anthony, I Lost Something

"Tony, Tony, turn around.

Something's lost and must be found."

St. Anthony, I know that you are the saint people pray to
   when they've lost something.

What a job you've got!

I lose things all the time!

My dad says that I'm "gifted" at losing socks, homework,
   library books, my glasses, and other stuff.

But this time, the thing I lost is really important.

Now, I'm pretty upset and nervous.

I've been praying that my search will have a happy
   ending.

Please help me to be patient,

to trust in God's goodness and your help.

Catherine Odell

When a Pet Is Lost

Gentle St. Francis,

My pet, _____, is lost. I'm afraid something bad
will happen. I'm afraid that my pet will never come
home. I miss my pet very much. Please watch over this
special friend of mine. Let some kind person take care of
my pet, and let us find my pet soon.

May God bless and take care of all animals. Amen.

Margaret Savitskas

Going to a New School

Dear Lord, soon I will have to move to another school. I
know that it's a big test for everyone who does it. It is
very hard to leave your friends and to try to
become part of a new class. At least, it is for
me. I hope that you will help me. Amen.

Sam, age 12, Russia

DID YOU kNOW

St. George was a brave Christian soldier in the Roman army. One famous story tells how he conquered a dragon to save the young people of a city. You may have some big, bad thing to fight against. It may be a sin like lying or talking back to your parents or picking on your little brother. It may be a bad habit, or a disability, or a sickness. You can ask St. George for help.

Prayer to St. George

Brave St. George,

I have a terrible dragon to fight. The dragon is

_____. Help me to be brave, to keep on fighting, to never give up, and to trust in God's help.

In the name of Jesus, help me to overcome this dragon in my life. Amen.

Margaret Savitskas

PRAYERS FOR GOD'S PRESENCE

Protection against Car Sickness

My family and I are going on a holiday, God,
and I am such a bad traveler . . .
Please help me not to get sick,
and to get there without feeling sick.
And please be with me
until the end of the journey.
Amen.

Shenuri, age 10, Sri Lanka

St. Teresa became a Carmelite nun in Spain. She saw that many changes were needed in convents to make them more pleasing to God. She traveled all over Spain, setting up new convents. Many people tried to stop what she was doing. Teresa had to rely on God to help her succeed.

Let Nothing Disturb You

Let nothing disturb you,

Let nothing frighten you.

All things pass.

God does not change.

Patience achieves everything.

Whoever has God lacks nothing.

God alone is enough.

St. Teresa of Ávila (1515–82)

You Are with Me

Dear Lord God,

You are everywhere.

When I am scared, I know you are with me.

When I fall down, I know you are with me.

I love you, Lord God.

Chloe, age 7

DID YOU kNOW St. Columba was born in Ireland. He made many journeys and founded more than a hundred monasteries. As a missionary, he brought the Christian faith to the people of Scotland.

Trust in God Alone

With you alone, my God,

I journey on my way.

I do not fear, when you are near,

O King of night and day.

More safe am I within your hand

Than if a crowd did round me stand.

St. Columba (521–97), adapted

PRAYERS FOR GOD'S GUIDANCE

Send out Your Light

God, send out your light and truth;

they will lead me on

and bring me to your holy mountain,

to your dwelling place.

Psalm 43:3, adapted

Prayer for a Difficult Time

God, I know that I ask for many things from you. Please
help me to pass through this difficult time. Or, at least, let
me be less worried. If there's anything that I hate, it's
being worried all the time. I hate that because I don't
know what will happen next. Please lead me through this
because you are my Light. You are my Light through this
dark moment of mine.

Patricio, age 13, Mexico

Serenity

God, grant me
The serenity to accept the things I cannot change,
The courage to change the things I can,
And the wisdom to know the difference.

Reinhold Niebuhr (1892–1971)

Save Us, God!

You who guided Noah over the floodwaters, hear us.

You who called Jonah back from the belly of the whale,
      deliver us.

You who saved Peter from sinking beneath the waves,
      help us.

Son of God, you did marvelous things of old.

Reach out in our day too.

> *Traditional prayer from Scotland,*
> *adapted*

Prayer for a Friend in Trouble

Dear God,

Please forgive this friend of mine who really doesn't want
      to do bad things but does.

Please help him to see the right way, your way.

Help him to be good like you, and help him to think
      about the things that he's been doing.

> *Daniel, age 14, Mexico*

PRAYERS FOR GOD'S PROTECTION

Guard Me

Guard me as the apple of the eye;
  hide me in the shadow of your wings.
Psalm 17:8

Your Guardian

The Lord is your guardian;
  the Lord is your shade at your right hand.
The sun shall not strike you by day,
  nor the moon by night.

The Lord will keep you from all evil;
  he will guard your life.
The Lord will guard
  your coming and your going,
  both now and forever.
Psalm 121:5–8, adapted

Prayer during a Winter Storm

Dear God,

the news says that

this blizzard could be the worst in decades.

I'm scared, and my parents are scared too.

Protect this house and all my family.

Protect my town and all people
>who don't have

warm clothes, extra food, or
>even good shelter.

Bring the homeless in and let
>every heart

be warm and open to them.

Catherine Odell

Prayer for Protection

May God who is great

Look upon me,

Have pity on me,

And grant me peace.

May God give me the strength and courage

That I may not be afraid.

For the angels of God are about me;

God is with me wherever I may be.

Traditional Jewish prayer

Be My Guardian and Guide

God, be my Guardian and Guide
And hear me when I call;
Let not my slippery footsteps slide
And hold me lest I fall.
And if I'm to weaken and sin
When selfish pride grows strong,
Please Lord, watch from within
And save my soul from wrong.

Isaac Williams (1802–65)

DID YOU kNOW
St. Patrick brought faith in God to people who believed in powerful pagan gods. It was a dangerous mission. Patrick called on the strength of the true God to protect and defend him.

In Time of Danger

May the strength of God pilot us.
May the power of God preserve us.
May the wisdom of God instruct us.
May the hand of God protect us.
May the way of God direct us.
May the shield of God defend us.

St. Patrick (c. 390–c. 461)

Prayer for Jungle Animals

We must keep nature going, dear Lord.

In seven or eight years,

all of the elephants in the jungles will be extinct.

The poachers must stop killing them for their ivory and
 the leopards for their skins.

The poachers also kill the bears by putting out honey,

and as the bear comes for the honey, they shoot it.

Dear Lord, tell the poachers not to shoot the poor animals.

They will be extinct very fast and that is too much of a sin.

Nishika, age 7, Sri Lanka

When I'm Far from Home

God, I'm worried when I am far from home and far from my parents. I'm afraid that something will happen to them and I won't see them again. Please, take care of them. Take care of me.

Juan Pablo, age 14, Mexico

Chapter 4
Prayers for Others

God Bless

God bless all those that I love;

God bless all those that love me;

God bless all those that love those that I love;

And all those that love those that love me.

Traditional New England blessing

PRAYERS FOR MY FAMILY

O Holy Family

O holy family—Jesus, Mary, and Joseph—
help my family to follow your example.
May we love each other as you did.
May we work together as you did.
May we do God's will in all things—as you did.
Amen.

Margaret Savitskas

Bless My Family

May the God of peace bless and protect my family.
May we follow Jesus in all that we do. Amen.

Mary, age 12

A Little Favor

God, I thank you because you have given me a GREAT family. I ask you to watch over my family through happiness and sorrow, when they are sad and lonely, and when we are having fun together. Please keep them safe so they don't get hurt. God, I ask you this little favor. Amen.

Kevin, age 10

For My Family's Safety

I pray that my family stays safe. I pray that they never get injured. I pray that they are happy and full of peace. I pray that when they do die they have lived a happy life. Amen.

Emily, age 9

Take Care of My Parents

Dear God, I love my parents very much. Please take good care of them and keep them healthy and safe. Please help them to do the right thing and to take good care of me and my brother.

Kelcy, age 8

Bless My Parents

Bless my parents and give them health. Take very, very good care of them, just like they take care of me.

Chelsea, age 8

Watch over My Parents

Watch over my parents as they get older. Guide them and send them good love. I hope we all stay together as long as we live. Send them prettiness and handsomeness. Amen.

Emily, age 9

DID YOU KNOW You can pray for your own father and mother every day. Ask Blessed Mary and St. Joseph to help them and pray for them too.

For My Father

Dear St. Joseph,

help my dad to be a good father.

Help him when he is tired,

when he is worried,

when he is in a hurry.

Give him pride in his work and

a little more time to have fun.

Help me to show my dad

how much I love him.

Amen.

Margaret Savitskas

For My Mother

Dear Blessed Mother Mary,

help my mom to be a good mother.

Give her peace and wisdom,

strength and courage,

grace and happiness.

Be nearby when she needs help.

Keep her close to your Son, Jesus.

Help me to always show my mom

how very much I love her.

Amen.

Margaret Savitskas

For My Twin

Dear God,

Thanks for giving me my brother. My twin is the first person I met. I love him. I wish I could be with him every second of the day. And if I can't be with him, may you be with him. I will care for him and be kind to him and pray for him. May you keep my brother safe. I love you, Lord. Amen.

Ian and Martin, age 9

DID YOU KNOW? St. Anselm was a great thinker and leader of the church. This is part of a longer prayer about God's love for us and our love for God and others.

For My Friends

O blessed Lord,

I ask your mercy for all people

but especially for the friends

you have given me. Amen.

St. Anselm of Canterbury
(c. 1033–1109)

For the House

Peace be to this house
And to all who live in it.
Peace to the people who enter
And to those who depart.

Traditional

Keep Us in Peace

O Lord, let your holy angels enter our home
and stay there to keep us in peace;
and may your blessing be upon us forever;
through Jesus Christ our Lord. Amen.

Traditional prayer of the church

PRAYERS FOR THE WORLD

For Families

Father, I pray for the families of all people on earth,

for the families of our nation,

for the families of my neighborhood,

and for my own family,

that we may all live in your peace.

May we know your love

and show your love

to the whole human family.

Margaret Savitskas

For Every Family on Earth

Lord God, Father of every family in heaven and on earth,
     you are Love and Life.

Through your Son, Jesus Christ, and through the Holy
     Spirit,

grant that every family on earth may be a place of life
     and love.

Grant that your grace may guide the thoughts and actions
     of husbands and wives for the good of their families.

Grant that children may find in their family support of
     their human dignity and growth in truth and love.

We ask this of you, Father, Son, and Spirit, who are Life,
     Truth, and Love. Amen.

Pope John Paul II

DID YOU kNOW Like Jesus, St. Peter Damian prayed for his friends. You can use this prayer or Jesus' prayer, John 17:6–26, to pray for people you know and those you don't know. You can pray about needs you know and about those that are known only to God.

For Many Others

Have mercy, Lord, on all my friends and relatives.

Have mercy, too, on all those who have tried to help me,

on all who pray for me,

and on all who have asked me to pray for them.

Give them your spirit,

pull all evil out by the roots,

and make them grow in many good ways.

Have mercy, Lord, on our bishops,

our pope,

our government leaders,

and on the whole Christian people.

Holy Mary, pray for them all.

All you saints of God, pray for them.

St. Peter Damian (1007–72), adapted

For the Children of the World

Almighty Father, I pray for the children of the whole world. Have mercy on them and comfort them. Help those who are sick, suffering from AIDS. I pray for those children on the streets who do not have homes and something to eat. I pray for those orphans who have lost their parents through diseases and wars. I pray for those who do not have money for school. Help them all, dear Father. Amen.

James, age 11, Uganda

A Prayer for Children

God our Father, you sent your only Son to earth to save us. He was once young like us. He loved little children like us. Help us to be like your Son, Jesus Christ. Help us to love our friends who are young like us. Help us to receive the sacraments and to do what is good. Amen.

Molly, age 9, Uganda

Bless the World with Peace

Dear Lord, Jesus Christ,

I ask forgiveness for the sins of today and of the past.

I ask that you bless the world with your love and hope.

I ask that you give peace throughout the world.

Meg, age 10

May the Road Rise to Meet You

May the road rise to meet you.

May the wind be always at your back.

May the sun shine warm upon your face.

May the rains fall softly upon your fields.

And, until we meet again,

May God hold you in the hollow of his hand.

Traditional Irish blessing

May God Fill Your Heart

May there always be work for your hands to do.

May your purse always hold a coin or two.

May the sun always shine upon your windowpane.

May a rainbow be certain to follow each rain.

May the hand of a friend always be near to you.

May God fill your heart with gladness to cheer you.

Traditional Irish blessing

For All Creatures

Dear Father, hear and bless

Your beasts and singing birds;

And guard with tenderness

Small things that have no words.

Traditional

For the Monkeys

Dear God,

Please take care of all the animals, but especially monkeys. They are my favorite animal in the world. They are so cute and cuddly with their nice fur. How old do they get?

Alex, age 8

Bless the Animals

Dios bendice a los animales
a los niños enfermos
a las plantas
y gracias por lo que nos das.
Amén.

God bless the animals
and the sick kids
and the plants
and thank you for all that you give us.
Amen.

Gabriela, age 9

PRAYERS FOR RELIGIOUS LEADERS AND TEACHERS

For Religious Leaders

God our Father, we thank you for our religious leaders.
We thank you for the good news they preach to us. Help
them give a good example. Give them words to preach.
Give them love to be shared. Bless and protect our pope,
cardinals, bishops, and priests. We pray all this through our
Lord, Jesus Christ. Amen.

Francis, age 10, Uganda

For Priests, Deacons, Brothers, and Sisters

God—Father, Son, and Holy Spirit—
bless all the men and women
who are priests, deacons, brothers, and sisters.
Thank you for these good people.
May they be faithful
in bringing your love to the world.
May they be happy
in serving your people.
Help others you are calling to work for you
to say YES!

Margaret Savitskas

For the Pope

The Lord preserve him and give him life,
  and make him blessed upon the earth,
  and deliver him not to the will of his
  enemies. Amen.

Traditional

For My Teacher

Thank you for my teacher. She is nice and funny and smart. She could be doing lots of other jobs. But I guess she wants to teach kids like me. I think that is great. Please give lots of good blessings to my teacher. And help all of her students to be good and to pay attention. Amen.

Andrew, age 11

 Elizabeth Ann Seton was a very good teacher and the mother of five children. She loved God so much that she became a saint. She was born in New York City.

Prayer to St. Elizabeth Ann Seton

I like my teacher. But sometimes my teacher gets mad when kids don't listen. I think it must be hard to be a good teacher. Please help my teacher to be a good teacher—to laugh more and yell less, to do a good job every day, and to love God. Amen.

Elizabeth, age 12

For Our Teachers

Lord God our Father, we thank you for giving us our
teachers. We thank you for the knowledge they feed us.
Give them life, let them live happily, and give them love
and strength. Let them teach us well so that we pass with
high grades in our exams. Amen.

Olivia, age 10, Uganda

PRAYERS FOR PEOPLE WHO ARE HARD TO LOVE

 DID YOU kNOW

Jesus said these words when he was dying on the cross. He
prayed for his enemies and for those who hurt him.

For Those Who Hurt Me

Father, forgive them; for they do not know what they
are doing.

Luke 23:34

For Those Who Are Hard to Love

Lord Jesus, you told us that we should love everyone. Even those kids who are mean to me, even those kids who make fun of me. Even those kids who are hard to like. Help me to forgive as you forgave those who hurt you. Help me to be kind to everyone. Help me to be loving. Amen.

Matthew, age 10

PRAYERS FOR PEOPLE WHO ARE HURTING

For a Lonely Person

Dear Lord, there is a new girl in our class who doesn't have any friends. All my friends seem to be ignoring her. Please help her to have many friends. Please Lord, help me to be able to make my friends friendly toward her. I thank you for giving me all my friends when I am lonely. In my loneliness you've always helped me. So, dear Lord, please help this girl too, and all the people who are lonely. Amen.

Shenuri, age 10, Sri Lanka

For Sick Children

Dear God,

I ask you to care especially for children who are sick, who cannot run and play. Give strength and wisdom to their parents, doctors, and nurses. Protect and bless all children with your mercy and love. Amen.

Maire, age 9

For a Sick Person

Jesus, you cured many people who were sick. You love and care for sick people. Someone I know is sick. This person's name is _____. Please take care of _____ and help him/her get better soon.

Juliana, age 9

For People in Need

Dear God,

I want everyone to have enough food to eat, clothes to wear, and a good place to live. I know some people don't have these things. I pray that they will not be too sad. Help them know that you love them. And I pray that they will have what they need. Please help me and all people to share the good things you have given us. I will give _____.

Anya, age 11, Russia

For Those Who Are Poor

Jesus,

I saw a homeless man on the street today. It made me feel sad. People were hurrying past him. No one paid attention to him. How can I help? Please let me know how I can help.

Zachary, age 9

Prayer to Be Generous

Dear God, thank you for the gifts you give me: my life, my friends, and best of all, my family. Some people wander around without any shelter, and some live their lives all alone. Please help people who have less than me. I have many gifts, but one of the best is the power to believe, and I thank you for that. Help me to share with others the love you give to me.

Kate, age 10

 DID YOU KNOW Mother Teresa took care of poor, sick, and dying people in the city of Calcutta, India. Today, her sisters, the Missionaries of Charity, follow her example in cities and countries around the world.

Make Us Worthy, Lord

Make us worthy, Lord,
To serve our fellow men
Throughout the world
Who live and die
In poverty or hunger.
Give them through our hands
This day their daily bread
And by our understanding love
Give peace and joy.

Mother Teresa of Calcutta (1910–97)

St. Joseph is the patron saint of people who are dying. Why? Because Jesus and Mary were probably with him when he died.

For People Who Are Dying

St. Joseph, I ask you to pray for all people who are dying. I pray that God will take away their pain and sadness and that they will be able to go to heaven soon. Be there with Mary and Jesus to welcome them when they come.

Margaret Savitskas

For Those Who Have Died

Eternal rest grant to them, O Lord,

and let your everlasting light shine upon them.

May they rest in peace.

Amen.

Traditional

PRAYERS FROM THE BIBLE

 Jesus greeted his friends with these words after he rose from the dead.

Peace be with you.

John 20:21

 This blessing was exchanged between Boaz and the reapers working in his field.

The Lord be with you.
The Lord bless you.

Ruth 2:4, adapted

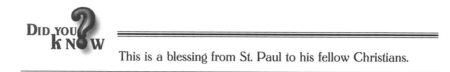

This is a blessing from St. Paul to his fellow Christians.

The grace of the Lord Jesus Christ, the love of God, and
the communion of the Holy Spirit be with all of you.

2 Corinthians 13:13

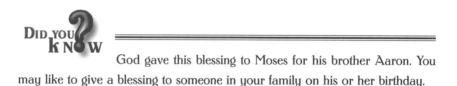

God gave this blessing to Moses for his brother Aaron. You
may like to give a blessing to someone in your family on his or her birthday.

The Lord bless you and keep you!

The Lord let his face shine upon you, and be gracious
to you!

The Lord look upon you kindly and give you peace!

Numbers 6:24–26, adapted

Chapter 5
Prayers for All Day and Night

The Moon Shines Bright

The moon shines bright,
The stars give light
Before the break of day;
God bless you all
Both great and small
And send you a joyful day.

Traditional

MORNING PRAYERS

Prayer to Start the Day

Dear Jesus,

send my guardian angel—

the one with the black hair, the brown eyes, the toasty

    skin, the rosebud lips, the rainbow dress, the fluttery

    wings, and the glowy halo—

to be with me all day long.

Keep me safe, healthy, kind, wise, and virtuous.

Take care of everyone I love

and everyone who needs your help. Amen.

Johanna, age 9

Blessed with Your Love

God, I pray that the day to come will be blessed with
your love.

Rachel, age 9

Rejoice and Be Glad

This is the day that the LORD has made;

let us rejoice and be glad in it.

Psalm 118:24

Morning Offering

Heavenly Father,

I offer you this day

All that I think or do or say,

Uniting it with what was done

By Jesus Christ, your only Son.

Amen.

Traditional, adapted

God's Little Bird

God's bird in the morning
I'll be!
I'll set my heart
within a tree
close to his bed
and sing to him
happily
a sunrise hymn.

*Traditional children's prayer from
England, adapted*

Help Me Be Strong

God, help me to be strong each day of my life, to give my
life a meaning, and not to live based upon what others
think and how they judge me. Let me wake up each
morning eager to start the new day.

Amado, age 12, Mexico

DID YOU KNOW You can get an idea of the great strength of God from the mighty forces of nature. Call on God each morning to guide you through the day. This prayer can help you remember that you depend on God for everything.

I Arise Today

I arise today

Through the strength of heaven:

Light of sun,

Radiance of moon,

Splendor of fire,

Speed of lightning,

Swiftness of wind,

Depth of sea,

Stability of earth,

Firmness of rock.

I arise today

Through God's strength to pilot me:

God's wisdom to uphold me,

God's eye to look before me,

God's ear to hear me,

God's word to speak to me,

God's hand to guide me,

God's way to lie before me,

God's angels to save me.

Attributed to St. Patrick (c. 390–c. 461)

In Your Sight

O Heavenly Father,

in whom I live and move and have my being,

I humbly pray that you guide me by your Holy Spirit,

that in all the cares and occupations

of this day, I will not forget you,

but remember that I am always walking in your sight.

Amen.

From an ancient opening prayer
of the Mass

DAYTIME PRAYERS

Teach Me Your Ways

Teach me your ways, Lord;

make your path known to me.

Lead me in your truth, and teach me,

for you are my God.

Psalm 25:4–5, adapted

Light My Path

Your word is a lamp to my feet

and a light to my path.

Psalm 119:105

Guide My Steps

O Christ,

keep me in your holiness

so that all day long

I may learn your goodness.

Make my path straight.

Guard my life.

Guide my steps,

through the prayers

of Mary, Mother of God,

and of all your saints.

Amen.

St. John Chrysostom
(c. 349–407), adapted

Give Me Courage

O God, give me the courage to stand up for what I believe in.

Samantha, age 9

DID YOU KNOW St. Teresa was a Spanish Carmelite nun. She wrote that prayer is friendship. Praying means taking time to build a friendship with the One who loves us.

Your Will Be Done

Lord, let me always be guided by you and follow your plan for me. Today and all the days of my life, help me to do what you want of me. May your will be done in all things, great and small. Amen.

St. Teresa of Ávila (1515–82), adapted

God, Be with Me

God be in my head
   and in my understanding.
God be in my eyes
   and in my looking.
God be in my mouth
   and in my speaking.
God be in my heart
   and in my thinking.
God be at my end
   and my departing.

Sarum Primer, 1527

A breastplate is armor that a soldier or warrior wore for protection. St. Patrick relied on the power of God for protection. Below is a part of his prayer.

The Breastplate of St. Patrick

I bind unto myself today
The power of God to hold and lead,
His eye to watch, his might to stay,
His ear to hearken to my need.
The wisdom of my God to teach,
His hand to guide, his shield to ward;
The word of God to give me speech,
His holy angels to be my guard.

Christ be with me, Christ within me,
Christ behind me, Christ before me,
Christ beside me, Christ to win me,
Christ to comfort and restore me,
Christ beneath me, Christ above me,
Christ in the hearts of all
who love me,
Christ in quiet, Christ in danger,
Christ in mouth of friend
and stranger.

St. Patrick (c. 390–c. 461)

For the Gift of Love

Thank you, Lord, for your grace and your love,

And all of the gifts you give from above.

Help me to show others your love every day,

In all that I do, and in all that I say.

Anonymous

DID YOU KNOW? St. Ignatius was a brave Spanish soldier. After he was wounded he became a priest and founded the Society of Jesus, or the Jesuits.

Prayer for a Generous Spirit

Dear Lord,

teach me to be generous.

Teach me to serve you as you deserve,

to give of myself

and not to ask for reward,

except the reward of knowing

that I am doing your will.

Amen.

St. Ignatius of Loyola (1491–1556)

DID YOU KNOW   St. Thomas More was a powerful man in the government in England. He was arrested and beheaded because he upheld the teaching of the church over the authority of the king.

Pray and Work

Lord Jesus Christ, be with me today.

And help me in all I think, and do, and say.

The things, good Lord, that we pray for,

give us grace to work for.

St. Thomas More (1478–1535)

Day by Day

Day by day, dear Lord,

three things I pray:

to see you more clearly,

love you more dearly,

follow you more nearly,

day by day.

St. Richard of Chichester
(c. 1197–1253)

Just for Today

I pray that I may be today
what you created me to be.

St. Thomas More (1478–1535)

With Love

Help me today, God,
to do ordinary things
with extraordinary love.

Mother Teresa of Calcutta (1910–97)

Be Near

Little angel of my God,
be always near to me.
When I play and when I work,
be always near to me.

Traditional children's prayer from Italy

Mary, Help Me

Mary, my mother,

you were filled with grace and love of God.

Help me to love God too.

You said yes when God asked you to be the mother of Jesus.

Help me to obey God too.

You hurried to visit your cousin Elizabeth.

Help me to be ready to help others too.

You gave birth to the Son of God in a stable.

Help me to bring Jesus to the world too.

You took care of Jesus every day when he was growing up.

Help me to stay close to Jesus too.

You walked with Jesus and stood at the foot of his cross.

Help me to follow Jesus too.

Margaret Savitskas

Mary, Pray for Me

Holy Mary, holy Mother, pray for me now.

Traditional

Jesus was tempted by the devil in the wilderness. Jesus was strong against temptation. He can help you to be strong and to show your love for God. You can read about how Jesus handled the devil in the Bible, in Matthew 4:1–11.

Prayer in Time of Temptation

Jesus, I do not want to sin. I know that a temptation is not a sin. It is a time for me to prove my love for you by not sinning. Give me grace to overcome temptation. I am weak, Jesus, but you are strong. With you, I will be strong. Amen.

Noah, age 11

When Jesus was a boy, he was obedient to Mary and Joseph. You can ask him to help you to obey your parents and those in authority. You can read about what happened to Jesus when he was twelve years old in Luke 2:41–52.

Prayer to Be Obedient

Loving Father, I am your child. I want to always obey your commandments. Help me to obey my parents and my teachers and others who are in charge of me. And that includes my big sister. And help my sister to be nice to me. Amen.

Alexei, age 10, Russia

Before Study

Holy Spirit, give me your gifts of
wisdom and understanding.
Help me to do my best on this work.
Fill my heart with Jesus, the light of the world.
Lead me to Jesus, the truth in all things.
Amen.

Luke, age 11

Before a Test

God, help me to do my best on this test. Please help me
to think clearly and to remember what I
studied. I offer you my work and my efforts.
Amen.

Analiese, age 11

Before a Basketball Game

Holy Spirit, guide me and help me to win. I would like
you to help me do my best, be safe, and have fun.

Michael, age 11

Before a Soccer Game

God, please help me to do my best in this game. Help me especially to be a good sport. Help me to play fairly and to be kind whether I win or lose. Protect me from injury and help me grow strong in body and spirit. Amen.

Lauren, age 10

A Swimmer's Prayer

God, please be with me through this race. Help me do my best and finish strong. And please don't let the water be too cold.

Danielle, age 9

St. Thomas Aquinas was a great thinker and writer. But he was humble enough to ask God to guide him.

When Going Out

Guide my going in and going forward,

lead home my going forth.

St. Thomas Aquinas (c. 1225–74)

 The archangel Raphael guided and protected a young man named Tobiah on a long journey. You can read this story in Tobit 5–12. Your guardian angel is ready to watch over you at all times.

Before a Trip

Archangel Raphael and my guardian angel,
Please watch over me and those I will travel with. Protect us from all danger and harm. Be with all the drivers and truckers on the highway so they don't have accidents. Bring us home safely. Amen.

Miguel, age 10

MEAL PRAYERS

You Give Us Food

By and by, you give us food,

by and by, we eat.

By and by, you nurture crops,

by and by, we harvest.

Brandon, age 10

A Garden Grace

Thank you, God, for our food and for the garden that
I have.

I love the food that grows in my garden.

Thank you, God, for the food that grows in every garden
in the world, because gardens and farms give us all food.

Kristie, age 10

You Feed the Birds

God, our loving Father,
you feed the birds of the sky
and clothe the lilies of the field.
We praise you for your creation.
We thank you for this meal
that you have given us.
We pray that no one will be
without food and care. Amen.

Margaret Savitskas

Prayer before a Meal

Bless us, O Lord,

and these your gifts,

which we are about to receive

from your bounty.

Through Christ our Lord.

Amen.

Traditional

Be Present, Lord

Be present at our table, Lord,

Be here and everywhere adored;

Thy creatures bless, and grant that we

May feast in paradise with thee.

John Cennick (1718–55)

Blessed Be God

Blessed be you, Lord God of the universe,
who brings forth bread from the earth
and makes glad the hearts of your people.

Ancient Hebrew prayer

Be Our Guest

Lord Jesus, be our guest,
Our morning prayer,
Our evening rest,
And with this daily food impart
Your love and grace to every heart.

Anonymous

We Thank You

We thank you, God, for happy hearts,
For rain and sunny weather;
We thank you, God, for this our food,
And that we are together.

Anonymous

Short Graces

God is great,
God is good,
And we thank God
For this food.

🌀

For health and strength and daily food,
we praise your name, O Lord.

🌀

May the food that we bless in your name, O Lord,
give us the strength to serve you.

🌀

Bless, O Lord, this food to our use
and ourselves to your service.

🌀

For every cup and plateful,
God, make us truly grateful.

🌀

For what we are about to receive
May the Lord make us truly thankful.
Amen.

Anonymous

Prayer after a Meal

We give you thanks, O Lord,

for all the graces and benefits

we have received from your bounty.

Through Christ our Lord.

Amen.

Traditional

NIGHT PRAYERS

 A mantle is a long cloak. Imagine how safe you would feel with Mary's mantle covering you like a warm blanket while you sleep.

An Evening Prayer

My God,

I thank you

for all the blessings you have given me

this day.

I offer you my sleep

and all the moments of this night.

I put myself in your hands

and under the mantle of our Lady.

Let your holy angels stand about me

and keep me in peace.

And let your blessing be on me.

Amen.

St. Alphonsus Liguori (1696–1787)

I Sleep in Peace

I will lie down and sleep in peace;

for you alone, O Lord, keep me safe.

Psalm 4:8, adapted

 These were the last words Jesus said before he died on the cross. With these words he gave himself to his Father. You can use Jesus' words to put yourself into God's hands before you go to sleep at night.

Prayer of Jesus

Father, into your hands I commend my spirit.

Luke 23:46

My Bedtime Prayer

My God, I lay me down to rest.
Maybe I didn't do my very best.
Help me through the day tomorrow
and please let there be no sorrow.
Help all people in the world today
and make the devil fade away.
Give us lots of peace and love,
I pray this to my God above.

Eric, age 9

A Prayer in My Heart

Jesus, keep me safe under the covers tonight. Please help
me not to have any bad dreams. I will go to sleep with a
prayer in my heart. Amen.

Lauren, age 10

My Work Is Done

O Lord, my day's work is finished;

Bless all that I have done right,

And forgive what I have done wrong;

And for the last minutes of this day,

Grant me the peace and rest

that come from you alone.

Franciscan prayer, adapted

In the Name of the Father

The peace of all peace be mine this night

+ In the name of the Father, the Son, and the Holy Spirit.

Amen.

+ *This means you make the sign of the cross.*

Traditional prayer from Ireland

Protect Us, Lord

Protect us, Lord, as we stay awake;

watch over us as we sleep,

that awake, we may keep watch with Christ,

and asleep, rest in his peace.

From the Night Prayer of the church

Keep Me Safe

Lord, keep me safe this night

And quiet all my fears;

O bless and guard me while I sleep

Till morning light appears.

Anonymous

Now I Lay Me Down to Sleep

Now I lay me down to sleep,

I pray you, Lord, your child to keep;

Your love be with me through the night

And wake me with the morning light.

Traditional

Don't Be Afraid

Four corners has my bed,

Four angels with wings outspread,

Two at my feet, two at my head.

The virgin Mary sings to me,

Rest and sleep, my child,

I am here, don't be afraid.

Traditional prayer from Mexico

God, Save Us

God, save us.

God, hide us.

When we sleep, God, do not sleep.

If we sleep, God, do not get drowsy.

Tie us around your arm, God,

like a bracelet.

Traditional prayer of the Sambura people,
Kenya

Grant Us Peace

May the all-powerful Lord

grant us a restful night

and a peaceful death. Amen.

From the Night Prayer of the church

Matthew, Mark, Luke, and John

Matthew, Mark, Luke, and John
Bless the bed that I lie on.
Before I lay me down to sleep
I give myself to God to keep.

Above the corners of my bed,
Angel wings open and spread,
One at my head, one at my feet,
And two to guard me while I sleep.

I go by sea, I go by land,
The Lord made me with his right hand.
If any danger comes to me,
O dear God, deliver me.

He is the branch and I am the flower,
May God bless my every hour.

Traditional children's prayer, adapted

Night Prayer

In my little bed I lie,
God my Father, hear my cry.
Please protect me through the night;
Keep me safe till morning light.
Amen.

Traditional children's prayer from Pakistan

Prayer for My Home

God bless this house from roof to floor.

The twelve apostles guard the door.

Four angels round my bed;

Gabriel stands at the head,

John and Peter at the feet,

All to watch me while I sleep.

Traditional

I See the Moon

I see the moon,

And the moon sees me.

God bless the moon,

And God bless me.

Traditional

DID YOU KNOW

In this prayer, you pray for all those who need God's care to make it through a long, dark night.

Watch, Lord

Watch, Lord,

with those who wake, or watch, or weep tonight,

and give your angels charge over those who sleep.

Tend your sick ones, O Lord Jesus.

Rest your weary ones.

Bless your dying ones.

Soothe your suffering ones.

Pity your afflicted ones.

Shield your joyous ones.

And all for your love's sake.

St. Augustine (354–430)

Chapter 6

Prayers for the Season and the Year

Listen!

If today you hear God's voice,
harden not your heart.

Psalm 95:7–8, adapted

PRAYERS FOR LENT AND EASTER

 This prayer is said on Ash Wednesday while ashes are traced on your forehead in the shape of a cross. The ashes are made from burned palms from the Passion (or Palm) Sunday of the previous year.

Ashes on Your Forehead

Remember, human, that you are dust,
and to dust you will return.

Genesis 3:19, adapted

Return to Me

Return to me, says the LORD of hosts, and I
will return to you.

Zechariah 1:3

Forty Days of Lent

God, do you see the cross of ashes on my forehead?
It will be washed away tomorrow.

But I hope that my Lenten promises to you won't
wash away so quickly:

1. Help me to fast a little from the foods and things I
really like.

2. Help me to share my money with the poor
and needy.

3. Help me to pray each day.

I've got forty days, God. Help me to spend them well.

Catherine Odell

Think of the Poor

Happy are those who consider the poor;
  the Lord saves them in times of trouble.
The Lord protects them and saves their lives;
  they are called happy on earth.

Psalm 41:1–2, adapted

What Wondrous Love Is This?

What wondrous love is this, O my soul, O my soul?
What wondrous love is this, O my soul?
What wondrous love is this that caused the Lord of bliss
To lay aside his crown for my soul, for my soul,
To lay aside his crown for my soul.

To God and to the Lamb, I will sing, I will sing,
To God and to the Lamb, I will sing.
To God and to the Lamb who is the great I AM
While millions join the theme, I will sing, I will sing,
While millions join the theme, I will sing.

And when from death I'm free, I'll sing on, I'll sing on,
And when from death I'm free, I'll sing on.
And when from death I'm free, I'll sing on and joyful be,
And through eternity, I'll sing on, I'll sing on,
And through eternity, I'll sing on.

American folk hymn

The Time of Singing

For now the winter is past,
    the rain is over and gone.
The flowers appear on the earth;
    the time of singing has come,
and the voice of the turtledove
    is heard in our land.

Song of Songs 2:11–12

On Easter Morning

Jesus, after three days,
Your lungs filled with air again.
Your heart began to beat joyfully.
You opened your eyes in the darkness of the tomb.
Quickly, angels came to unbind your burial clothes.
Light, light, light!
Your tomb was pulsing with light and joy.
The stone broke free and you came out.
You conquered death, as you promised.
Your resurrection freed us all.
Alleluia, Jesus. Alleluia.

Catherine Odell

We Adore Thee

We adore you, O Christ, and we bless you because by your holy cross, you have redeemed the world.

Traditional Lenten prayer, adapted

Easter

The air is like a butterfly
  With frail blue wings.
The happy earth looks at the sky
  And sings.

Joyce Kilmer (1886–1918)

STATIONS OF THE CROSS

Praying the Stations of the Cross—alone or with a group—is a Lenten tradition. Read and pray these stations very slowly. Imagine the scene in Jerusalem as Jesus walked his Way of the Cross. Often, the Stations of the Cross is an action prayer. Catholics walk to the fourteen stations of the Way of the Cross and stop to pray at each one. The stations can be displayed outside in a park but are usually found inside churches.

Station 1. Jesus is condemned.

Jesus, you aren't guilty of any crime or sin. How can you be condemned? But the unthinkable happens. The people yell: "Crucify him! Crucify him!" Pilate finally agrees.

Station 2. Jesus receives the cross.

The cross is heavy and it hurts so much when it is slung across your back. Your back is raw from the beating. You begin to carry your cross, Jesus.

Station 3. Jesus falls the first time.

You fall to the ground beneath your heavy burden. Pain pierces every part of your body. The bystanders mock you, Jesus.

Station 4. Jesus meets his mother.

Your heart breaks when you see your mother's face. She feels every pain you feel. You say good-bye to your mother.

Station 5. Simon helps Jesus carry the cross.

Simon of Cyrene doesn't want your cross, Jesus. The soldiers make him help you. You are grateful and struggle to move up the hill a little faster.

Station 6. Veronica wipes the face of Jesus.

This woman wipes away the bloody sweat on your suffering face. It is an act of kindness, and you are so grateful. The image of your pain stains her cloth.

Station 7. Jesus falls the second time.

The narrow street up the steep hill toward Golgotha is difficult. Jesus, you fall again to your bloody knees. It is so difficult to get up again. But you do.

Station 8. Jesus meets the women of Jerusalem.

Do you know all of these weeping women, Jesus? They know you as the "man of sorrow," as an innocent lamb being led to slaughter. You try to console them.

Station 9. Jesus falls the third time.

This time, your face hits the hard stone street. Your head throbs with pain, and you are dizzy with it. Obediently, you get up to travel on to the hill of crucifixion.

Station 10. Jesus is stripped of his clothing.

No care and no dignity is given to you now, Jesus. Even your clothes are taken. You have nothing left to give except suffering and your final breaths.

Station 11. Jesus is nailed to the cross.

Wrists first and then your feet. Long iron spikes nail you to the cross. Then the cross is hauled up for the world to see. I'm so sorry, Jesus.

Station 12. Jesus dies.

In your last hours, your suffering is so great. You call to your Father. You feel abandoned. After a few more words, you release your last breath.

Station 13. Jesus is taken down from the cross.

Jesus, now you can feel no pain. No hateful statements or lies can wound you. Soldiers pull out the spikes and release your body from the cross.

Station 14. Jesus is laid in the tomb.

In a hurry, your body is wrapped and laid on a cold stone. You have a borrowed grave, Jesus. The sun goes down and your body grows cold in the darkness.

The Feast of the Resurrection

On the third day after your death, you rise again. Jesus, you return to life in glory. Death could not hold you. Alleluia, alleluia. Jesus is risen.

Adapted for children by Catherine Odell

PRAYERS FOR ADVENT AND CHRISTMAS

 This is a prayer that Christians pray during Advent, when they are waiting for Jesus to come at Christmas. You can pray it any time you are longing for Jesus. The word "maranatha" is Aramaic and means "O Lord, come."

Maranatha (Come, Lord)

Come, Lord Jesus. Come quickly!

1 Corinthians 16:22, adapted

Jesus, Come Again: An Advent Prayer

Jesus, you were born in Bethlehem
    and lived in Nazareth.
You grew up tall and straight,
    smiling and smelling
    the tangy sawdust
    from Joseph's chisel and saw.

Later, you left your home and everything you knew.
Your Father's work was waiting
    and you knew it had to be done.
You gathered friends around you,
    but alone you suffered and died.

That cold, dark tomb couldn't hold you
   because you are the Son of God.

Jesus, come again,
   come into my heart at Christmas.
I'm waiting for you this Advent.
In sleepy Nazareth, before your birth,
   Mary fashioned squares of cloth.
She wrapped your tiny, shivering body
   in those warm swaddling clothes.
I will welcome you too, tiny Jesus,
   wrapping my love tightly around you.

Catherine Odell

Jesus, the Dayspring

O come, O Dayspring from on high

And cheer us by your drawing nigh;

Disperse the gloomy clouds of night,

And death's dark shadow put to flight.

Latin hymn from the ninth century

 A rite is a set of special prayers, ceremonies, and worship traditions. Prayers of the Roman rite were used in Western Europe and in Rome in the first centuries.

The Son of God Once Came

You believe that the Son of God once came to us;

You look for him to come again.

May his coming bring you the light of his holiness

And free you with his blessing.

From the Roman rite

Sign of the Redeemer

Therefore the Lord himself will give you a sign. Look, the young woman is with child and shall bear a son, and shall name him Immanuel.

Isaiah 7:14

 In December 1531, the Blessed Virgin Mary appeared to fifty-seven-year-old Juan Diego near Mexico City. Today, you can still see Juan's cloak, where a picture of Our Lady of Guadalupe mysteriously appeared. It is kept in a church in Mexico City. The feast of Blessed Juan Diego is December 9. The feast of Our Lady of Guadalupe is December 12.

Prayer to Our Lady of Guadalupe

Dearest Mary, Our Lady of Guadalupe,

many years ago, in Mexico,

you came to visit the Indian Juan Diego.

High on a hill, you visited him.

You told Juan that he and his poor people

were God's precious sons and daughters.

You gave to Juan a beautiful portrait of yourself.

In a strange and wonderful way, it was painted on his
   rough cloak.

Help me to always remember how much I too am loved.

Put a picture of yourself in my heart.

Catherine Odell

"Las posadas" is Spanish for "the shelters." In Mexico and in the Southwest, Las Posadas is observed from December 16 to December 24. The people reenact the journey to Bethlehem and celebrate with songs, prayers, special foods like tamales and donuts, and a chocolate drink called "champurrados." The tradition started in Mexico in 1587.

A Journey with Mary and Joseph

In my heart, Mary and Joseph, I will journey with you
    and others for "Las Posadas."
Carrying lanterns, we sing joyfully and walk along with
    brave Joseph.
He leads poor, tired Mary on her little donkey.
From house to house we go, asking to come in, to find a
    quiet place for the young mother who is about to
    give birth.
"We have no room. There's no room for you!"
On and on, we travel in hope, following an angel.
Finally, on the ninth night, on December 24, we find
    shelter for the holy pilgrims.
Your holy child is born in a borrowed stable.
We will feast and sing and rejoice.
The long, hard journey has ended.
This newborn child shall bring us so much joy.

Catherine Odell

What Can I Give Him?

What can I give him,
Poor as I am?
If I were a shepherd,
I would bring a lamb.
If I were a wise man,
I would do my part —
Yet what can I give him,
Give him my heart.

Christina Rossetti (1830–94)

O Child So Wise

Jesus Christ, O Child so wise,
bless my hands and fill my eyes,
and bring my soul to Paradise.

Hilaire Belloc (1870–1953), adapted

What Child Is This?

What child is this,
   who, laid to rest,
   on Mary's lap is sleeping?
Whom angels greet
   with anthems sweet,
   while shepherds watch are keeping?

Why lies he in
   such mean estate,
   where ox and ass are feeding?
Good Christian, fear
   for sinners here,
   the silent word is pleading.

So bring him incense,
   gold and myrrh.

Come peasant, king
  to own him.
The king of kings,
  salvation brings;
  let loving hearts enthrone him.

This, this is Christ the King,
  whom shepherds guard
  and angels sing:
Haste, haste to bring him laud,★
  the babe, the son of Mary.

★*laud*—praise

Traditional English Christmas carol

Christmas Eve Prayer

Thank you, Lord my God, for letting us celebrate your
  birthday with beautiful lights and a Christmas tree.
This day is special to me.
Help me to go to sleep this Christmas Eve night.
It's hard to sleep because I'm excited about
  opening the gifts that you give to me. Amen.

Haley, age 10

The Angels' Song

Glory to God in the highest heaven,
   and on earth peace among those whom he favors!

Luke 2:14

Rabbits for the Little Child

Señora doña Maria,
I come from far away.
I bring a pair of rabbits
To the little Child today.

Squash, I bring, potatoes,
And flour for your bread.
I came to see your family,
Your baby in his bed.

Above this barn in Bethlehem
Stars light the sky in awe,
The Virgin and St. Joseph
And the Savior in the straw.

Traditional prayer from Chile, adapted

Silent Night

Silent night, holy night!

All is calm, all is bright.

Round yon Virgin, Mother and Child,

Holy Infant, so tender and mild.

Sleep in heavenly peace,

Sleep in heavenly peace.

Silent night, holy night!

Shepherds quake at the sight.

Glories stream from heaven afar,

Heavenly hosts sing Alleluia,

Christ the Savior is born!

Christ the Savior is born!

Silent night, holy night!

Son of God, love's pure light.

Radiant beams from Thy holy face,

With the dawn of redeeming grace,

Jesus, Lord at Thy birth,

Jesus, Lord at Thy birth.

Joseph Mohr (1792–1848) and
Franz Gruber (1787–1863)

PRAYERS FOR OTHER CELEBRATIONS

Yeah! It's My Birthday!

Hey, God, it's my birthday today!
It's finally here!
Thanks for everything that
will come my way today.
Presents and candles on my cake—
I hope it's chocolate.
Birthday cards and hugs
and whatever I want for dinner.
Thanks for the gift of life, God.
I'm glad to be alive. I'm glad to be me.
You picked out my birthday, and it's a great one!
Thanks for my family, my home, my friends,
and for every reason under the sun to say:
"Yeah, it's my birthday today!"

Catherine Odell

Birthday Thank-You

Dear God,

Thank you for my birthday. Thank you for all of your gifts to me: my family and my home, my friends and cousins. Thank you for food and water, for animals, flowers, and trees. Thank you for your love and care. I want to learn about you so that I can tell others about you.

Jacquee, age 9

One Year Older

Dear God,

I'm one year older now. It's my birthday. Thank you for bringing me closer to you this year.

Nick, age 9

A Sunday Prayer

Dear God,

I love Sundays, because on Sundays I go to Mass.

I spend extra time with you then.

Every Sunday, I pray to you.

Samantha, age 8

Prayer for Valentine's Day

Thanks, Lord, for giving me a heart to love with and a
brain to think with.

With these, I can love every person and I can think of
what they need.

Teach me to love everybody like you love me.

Rodrigo, age 13, Mexico

With All My Heart

Dear God,

It's Valentine's Day.

Help me to show my love today to those who need it
most.

I love my family and I love my friends.

But help me to let them know about my love.

Help me also to love at least one person who is a little bit
hard to love.

I will give valentines through my kind words, my actions,
my smile.

And don't let me forget to say,

"I love you, God . . . with all my heart!"

Catherine Odell

On My First Day of School

God, please help me with my studies this year.

Bless my classmates and my teacher so that they may all
do well.

God, just stay with us all year long. Amen.

Kellen, age 10

A Halloween Prayer

From Ghoulies and Ghosties,

Long-leggety Beasties,

and THINGS

that go BUMP in the night,

Good Lord, deliver us!

Anonymous

Thanksgiving Grace

Thank you for the turkey,

Thank you for the beets,

Thank you for the carrots,

Now let's start to eat.

Brandon, age 10

Thanksgiving—A Time to Share

Please God, let us have a good Thanksgiving.

If there are leftovers, let people eat them for the next dinner.

Let there be enough food for everybody. Amen.

Greg, age 8

First Snowfall

I'm so happy and excited, God,

As your delicate snowflakes fall . . .

Lazy and light,

Quiet as night,

Your snow makes no noises at all.

Flakes as big as a squirrel's paw

Soon cover the ground below.

The green disappears,

Maybe for years,

Asleep below blanketing snow.

Into my hands fall lace crystals,

Tiny cold kisses of white.

Snow on my nose,

Winter now blows;

It's your season of frozen delight.

Catherine Odell

Chapter 7

Traditional Prayers

Morning Offering

O Jesus, through the Immaculate Heart of Mary,

I offer you all of my prayers, works, joys, and sufferings of
this day,

for all the intentions of your Sacred Heart,

in union with the holy Sacrifice of the Mass throughout
the world,

in reparation for my sins,

for the intentions of all our associates,

and in particular for _____.

PRAYERS OF FAITH AND DEVOTION

Come, Holy Spirit

Come, Holy Spirit, fill the hearts of your faithful ones, and set them on fire with your love.

Verse: Send forth your Spirit and they shall be created.

Response: And you will renew the face of the earth.

God, you teach the hearts of the faithful by giving them the light of your Holy Spirit. Grant to us that, by your Spirit, we may be truly wise, and always experience the joy of your strengthening presence. Through Christ our Lord. Amen.

Act of Contrition

My God,

I am sorry for my sins with all my heart.

In choosing to do wrong

and failing to do good,

I have sinned against you

whom I should love above all things.

I firmly intend, with your help,

to do penance,

to sin no more,

and to avoid whatever leads me to sin.

Our Savior Jesus Christ

suffered and died for us.

In his name, my God, have mercy.

DID YOU KNOW "Confiteor" means "I confess" in Latin. The title comes from the first words of the prayer.

The Confiteor

I confess to almighty God

and to you, my brothers and sisters,

that I have sinned through my own fault,

in my thoughts and in my words,

in what I have done,

and in what I have failed to do.
And I ask blessed Mary, ever virgin,
all the angels and saints,
and you, my brothers and sisters,
to pray for me to the Lord our God.

The "suscipe" (sou-she-pā) is a traditional prayer of offering. In this prayer, you offer the Lord all of you.

Suscipe

Take, Lord, and receive all my liberty, my memory, my understanding and my entire will, all I have and call my own. You have given all to me. To you, Lord, I return it. Everything is yours; do with it what you will. Give me only your love and your grace, that is enough for me.

An Act of Faith

My God, I believe that you are one God in three persons: Father, Son, and Holy Spirit. I believe in Jesus Christ, your Son, who became man and died for our sins. I believe Jesus will come to judge the living and the dead. I believe all you teach us through the Catholic Church, because you teach the truth. Amen.

An Act of Hope

My God, I trust in your goodness and promises. I hope
for forgiveness of my sins, the help of your grace, and life
everlasting. I put my hope in Jesus Christ, my Lord and
Redeemer. Amen.

An Act of Love

My God, I love you above all things because you are
good and worthy of all my love. I love my neighbor as
myself for love of you. I forgive all who have injured me,
and I ask pardon of all whom I have
injured. Amen.

PRAYERS OF THE ROSARY

 The rosary is a series of prayers that is often said while holding a string of beads. The beads help the people praying to count the prayers. The Sign of the Cross, the Apostles' Creed, the Our Father, the Hail Mary, and the Glory Be are said during the rosary. Those praying the rosary think about mysteries, or great events in the life of Jesus and Mary, while they pray.

The Rosary

The Joyful Mysteries

1. The angel Gabriel tells Mary that she will be the mother of Jesus.

2. Mary visits her cousin Elizabeth.

3. Jesus is born.

4. Mary and Joseph present the baby Jesus to God in the temple.

5. Mary and Joseph find the child Jesus with the teachers in the temple.

The Sorrowful Mysteries

1. Jesus prays and suffers in the garden.

2. Jesus is beaten.

3. Jesus is crowned with thorns.

4. Jesus carries his cross.

5. Jesus dies on the cross.

The Glorious Mysteries

1. Jesus rises to life from death.

2. Jesus returns to his Father in heaven.

3. The Holy Spirit comes upon the disciples.

4. Mary is taken up into heaven.

5. Mary is crowned Queen of Heaven and Earth.

The Sign of the Cross

In the name of the Father,
and of the Son,
and of the Holy Spirit.
Amen.

The Apostles' Creed

I believe in God,

the Father almighty,

creator of heaven and earth.

I believe in Jesus Christ,

his only Son, our Lord.

He was conceived by the power of the Holy Spirit

and born of the Virgin Mary.

He suffered under Pontius Pilate,

was crucified, died, and was buried.

He descended to the dead.

On the third day he rose again.

He ascended into heaven,

and is seated at the right hand of the Father.

He will come again to judge the living and the dead.

I believe in the Holy Spirit,

the holy Catholic Church,

the communion of saints,

the forgiveness of sins,

the resurrection of the body,

and the life everlasting. Amen.

Glory Be

Glory to the Father,
and to the Son,
and to the Holy Spirit:
as it was in the beginning,
is now,
and will be forever. Amen.

The Lord's Prayer

Our Father, who art in heaven,
hallowed be thy name;
thy kingdom come;
thy will be done on earth as it is in heaven.
Give us this day our daily bread;
and forgive us our trespasses
as we forgive those who trespass against us;
and lead us not into temptation,
but deliver us from evil.
Amen.

The Hail Mary

Hail Mary,
full of grace,
the Lord is with you.
Blessed are you among women,
and blessed is the fruit of your womb, Jesus.
Holy Mary, mother of God,
pray for us sinners,
now and at the hour of our death.
Amen.

PRAYERS TO MARY

Hail, Holy Queen

Hail, holy Queen, Mother of mercy;
hail, our life, our sweetness, and our hope.
To you we cry, the children of Eve;
to you we send up our sighs,
mourning and weeping in this land of exile.
Turn, then, most gracious advocate,
your eyes of mercy toward us;
lead us home at last
and show us the blessed fruit of your womb, Jesus:
O clement, O loving, O sweet Virgin Mary.

The Memorare

Remember, most loving Virgin Mary,
never was it heard
that anyone who turned to you for help
was left unaided.

Inspired by this confidence,
though burdened by my sins,
I run to your protection
for you are my mother.

Mother of the Word of God,
do not despise my words of pleading
but be merciful and hear my prayer.
Amen.

The Angelus

The angel spoke God's message to Mary,
and she conceived of the Holy Spirit.
Hail Mary. . . .

"I am the lowly servant of the Lord:
let it be done to me according to your word."
Hail Mary. . . .

And the Word became flesh
and lived among us.
Hail Mary. . . .

Pray for us, holy Mother of God,
that we may become worthy of the promises of Christ.

Let us pray.

Lord,
fill our hearts with your grace:
once, through the message of an angel
you revealed to us the incarnation of your Son;
now, through his suffering and death
lead us to the glory of his resurrection.

We ask this through Christ our Lord.
Amen.

A litany is a series of requests. In this litany, we use the many different names for Mary to ask her to pray for us. If you pray this in a group, one person can say the name for Mary, and everyone else can say "Pray for us" together. You'll also find another litany in this chapter, a litany of the saints.

Litany of the Blessed Virgin Mary

Say "Pray for us" after each of the names for Mary.

Holy Mary, pray for us.

Holy Mother of God,

Holy virgin of virgins,

Mother of Christ,

Mother of the Church,

Mother of our Savior,

Virgin most powerful,

Virgin most merciful,

Virgin most faithful,

Cause of our joy,

Mystical Rose,

House of Gold,

Ark of the Covenant,

Gate of Heaven,

Morning Star,

Health of the sick,

Refuge of sinners,

Comforter of the suffering,

Help of Christians,
Queen of angels,
Queen of apostles,
Queen of martyrs,
Queen of all saints,
Queen of families,
Queen of Peace,
Pray for us, O holy Mother of God.

Prayer to the Virgin

We turn to you for protection,
holy Mother of God.
Listen to our prayers
and help us in our needs.
Save us from every danger,
glorious and blessed Virgin.

Sub Tuum Praesidium, *a prayer from
the third century*

PRAYERS TO SAINTS AND ANGELS

Prayer to a Guardian Angel

Angel of God, my guardian dear,

To whom God's love entrusts me here,

Ever this day be at my side,

To light and guard, to rule and guide.

Amen.

According to tradition, some angels rebelled against God. The archangel Michael was the leader of the angels who were loyal to God. St. Michael fought against Satan and his followers and threw them out of heaven. You can read about the battle in Revelation 12:7–9. Call on mighty St. Michael to defeat the forces of evil in the world today.

Prayer to St. Michael

St. Michael the archangel, defend us in the day of battle; guard us against the wickedness and tricks of the devil. By the power of God, throw into hell Satan and all the other evil spirits who prowl about the world, seeking the ruin of souls. Amen.

Adapted for children

Peace Prayer of St. Francis

Lord, make me an instrument of your peace:

where there is hatred, let me sow love;

where there is injury, pardon;

where there is doubt, faith;

where there is despair, hope;

where there is darkness, light;

and where there is sadness, joy.

O Divine Master, grant that I may not so much seek

to be consoled, as to console;

to be understood, as to understand;

to be loved, as to love.

For it is in giving that we receive,

it is in pardoning that we are pardoned,

and it is in dying that we are born to eternal life.

St. Francis of Assisi (c. 1181–1226)

Litany of the Saints

Say "Pray for us" after calling on each of the saints.

Holy Mary, pray for us.

St. Michael,

St. Gabriel,

St. Raphael,

Holy angels of God,

St. Joseph,

St. John the Baptist,

St. Peter,

St. Paul,

St. Andrew,

St. John,

All you holy apostles,

St. Stephen,

St. Lawrence,

St. Vincent,

All you holy martyrs,

St. Gregory,

St. Augustine,

All you holy bishops,

St. Anthony,

St. Benedict,

St. Dominic,

St. Francis,

All you holy priests and monks,

St. Mary Magdalene,

St. Agnes,

St. Cecilia,

St. Anastasia,

St. Catherine,

St. Teresa,

St. Thérèse,

All you holy saints of God,

(You may add the name of your own patron saint, the name of any saint you know and love, and the names of people in your family.)

Chapter 8
Prayers When I'm in Church

A Server's Prayer

Heavenly Father,

Please be with me today as I serve at Mass. Thank you for giving me the great opportunity to serve you this day. Help me remember that as I serve the priest, I am also serving you.

Please help me today so I will not do wrong, in church and later at home.

Amen.

Adam, age 11

Pray this psalm on Sunday when you are waiting for Mass to start. Or recite it for your family in the car on the way to church!

Worship the Lord

O come, let us sing to the LORD;

   let us make a joyful noise to the rock of our salvation!

Let us come into his presence with thanksgiving;

   let us make a joyful noise to him with songs of praise!

For the LORD is a great God,

   and a great King above all gods.

In his hand are the depths of the earth;

   the heights of the mountains are his also.

The sea is his, for he made it,

   and the dry land, which his hands have formed.

O come, let us worship and bow down,

   let us kneel before the LORD, our Maker!

For he is our God,

   and we are the people of his pasture,

   and the sheep of his hand.

Psalm 95:1–7

Prayer for Others

Jesus, I pray for the sick, the homeless, and families that go through hard times. Help them be healthy and pray to you. I pray for everyone, even families that don't go to church. Let them be able to talk to you while having trouble. Amen.

Tracey, age 9

 DID YOU KNOW You can say this prayer before the priest reads the Gospel. You can also say it at home before you read the Bible.

The Word of God

May the word of God
+ be in my thoughts
+ and on my lips
+ and in my heart.

+ Make a little cross, first on your forehead, then on your lips, and finally on your heart.

Traditional

Say this prayer when you are waiting to receive Jesus in Holy Communion. It is a good prayer to learn by heart.

Prayer before Holy Communion

Jesus, I believe in you,

I hope in you,

I love you.

Jesus, I am sorry for my sins.

Make my heart ready for you.

Come, Lord Jesus.

Margaret Savitskas

Elizabeth Ann Seton was thirty years old when she became a Catholic and received her first Communion. You can tell how happy it made her. You can use her prayer on your first Communion day or any time you welcome Jesus in Communion.

Prayer for First Communion Day

At last, my God, you are mine and I am yours. To my last breath of life I will remember waiting for this day. You have entered the little dwelling of my heart; it is all yours. You are like a king who has come to take his throne. I

am filled with joy and gladness. My heart dances within
me. I feel richer than a queen.

St. Elizabeth Ann Seton
(1774–1821), adapted

Prayer after Holy Communion

O Lord Jesus,
May your Body,
  which I have received,
  be ever close to my heart.
May your Blood,
  which I have received,
  keep me free from sin.
Stay with me always.
Make my heart like your heart:
  obedient to my heavenly Father
      and kind to others. Amen.
Margaret Savitskas

A Prayer of Thanksgiving

Thank you, Jesus, my friend, my savior, my Lord, my God,
for all that you have done for me.
For the blessings you give me,
I thank you, because they teach me about your love.
For joy and happiness,
I thank you, because I can share them with others.
Even for troubles and sadness,
I thank you, because I can share them with you.
For my family and friends,
I thank you, because they teach me how to love.
For coming to me in Holy Communion,
Jesus, I thank you, I love you.
Help me to remember that everything I have comes
    from you.

Margaret Savitskas

I Love You

Jesus, now that I have received you, I feel closer to you. I
feel warmer, I feel happy, and I have no doubt in your
greatness. Your heart is so full of compassion. You love
everyone, and I love you too. Amen.

Santiago, age 13, Mexico

Prayer of St. Peter

Lord; you know that I love you.

John 21:16

My Offering

Jesus, you have come into my heart.

You are my friend;

I welcome you.

You are God;

I adore you.

Jesus, you gave your life for me;

I thank you.

I offer you myself in return:

my mind to think of you,

my heart to love you,

my body to work for you,

my soul to praise you,

forever and ever. Amen.

Margaret Savitskas

I Am So Happy

Jesus,

I am so happy

that you have come to me today,

and I have so much to say.

(Now talk to Jesus in your own words.)

Margaret Savitskas

Jesus, I Am Yours

May the Body and Blood

of our Lord, Jesus Christ,

lead me to heaven.

Jesus, for you I live.

Jesus, for you I die.

Jesus, I am yours

while I live and when I die.

Traditional

Thank You, Jesus

How can I ever thank you

for all you have done for me?

I want to say,

thank you, Jesus,

a hundred thousand times.

Austin, age 11

Jesus is the Lamb of God. The blood of the lamb saved the Israelites. The blood of Jesus on the cross saves all people.

Lamb of God

Here is the Lamb of God who takes away the sin of the world!

John 1:29

 With these words, the Roman centurion (officer) showed his faith in Jesus. Then Jesus cured the man's servant. In the Mass, we pray a prayer like this. We say it before we receive Holy Communion. In it, we ask Jesus to heal us of sin.

Lord, I Am Not Worthy

Lord, I am not worthy to have you come under my roof; but only speak the word, and my servant will be healed.

Matthew 8:8

Love Enters In

God, grant what we take at your table
will now let your love enter in,
so the life that is lived in this moment
remains forever within.

Anonymous

DID YOU KNOW Thomas, the apostle, said this to Jesus when Jesus appeared to his friends after the Resurrection. Thomas was saying that he believed Jesus was God. You can say this prayer when Jesus comes to you.

Prayer of St. Thomas

My Lord and my God!

John 20:28

 DID YOU KNOW Julian was a holy woman in England. She wanted to be close to Jesus in the Blessed Sacrament all the time. So she lived in a room built right next to a church. It had a small window so she could see the altar and the tabernacle.

You Are Enough for Me

God, of your goodness,

give me yourself,

for you are enough for me,

and I can ask for nothing less

which can pay you full worship.

And if I ask for anything less

always I am in want,

but only in you do I have everything.

Julian of Norwich (c. 1342–c. 1420)

I Want to Love You More

I love you, O God,

and I want to love you more and more.

St. Anselm of Canterbury

(c. 1033–1109)

 DID YOU KNOW

St. Bernard was born in a castle in France. When he was twenty-two, this charming young nobleman vowed to serve Jesus alone. He became a leader of a monastery and a leader of the church of his time.

Jesus, My King

O King of Peace, come and reign in me,

for I will have no king but thee.

St. Bernard of Clairvaux (1090–1153)

Give Me, Lord

Give me, good Lord,

in all my works

and all my words

and all my thoughts,

a taste of your holy, blessed Spirit—

to be humble, peaceful, patient, and kind.

Give me, good Lord,

full faith,

firm hope,

and fervent charity—

love of you far above the love of myself.

St. Thomas More (1478–1535),
adapted

Imagine exploring a beautiful coral reef under water. St. Catherine's experience of praying was like being underwater, except she was covered by the mystery of God.

Deep into God

You, Father, Son, and Holy Spirit,

are like a deep sea.

The more I enter,

the more I find,

and the more I find,

the more I seek.

St. Catherine of Siena (1347–80)

Fruit of the Spirit

Fill our hearts, we pray you, with love, joy, peace,

patience, gentleness, goodness, faith,

meekness, and temperance, that we may

be your children, our Father.

St. Anselm of Canterbury

(c. 1033–1109)

Prayer before a Crucifix

Good and gentle Jesus,

I kneel before you.

I see your five wounds.

They have pierced your hands and feet.

They have hurt all your bones.

Fill my heart with faith, hope, and love.

Help me to be sorry for my sins,

and to turn my life to you.

Amen.

Traditional, adapted for children

Prayer before the Blessed Sacrament

Jesus, I believe you are present here

in this host of bread.

I believe it

because you said it is so.

The priest said your own words:

"This is my Body."

Jesus, I believe in you

and I trust in your promises.

You said that you are the bread of life.

Whoever eats this bread

will have eternal life.

I hope that someday

I will be with you forever
in heaven.
Jesus, I hope in you.
I love you more
than anything in the world.
I love you with my whole heart,
my whole soul,
my whole mind,
and my whole strength.
Help me to love my neighbor as myself.
I forgive all who have hurt me.
Please help those I have hurt to forgive me.
Jesus, help me to love you
more and more.

Margaret Savitskas

A Visit with Jesus

Jesus, long ago, parents brought their children to see you. You were very happy to see them! You welcomed those children. You smiled at them, put your arms around them, and blessed them.

Jesus, my parents have brought me here today to see you. I know you won't hug me in the same way. But still I feel your love. I know that you welcome me. You want me to come and spend some time with you. I am glad to be here, Jesus. I will tell you everything that is in my heart. (Now talk to Jesus from your heart.)

Jesus, bless me today as you blessed the children so long ago. And please bless my parents too.

Margaret Savitskas

DID YOU KNOW When Katharine was eight years old, her heart was set on two things: chocolate candy to share with her sisters and receiving Jesus in Holy Communion. Her mother did not approve of sweets, but Katharine got her first wish for Christmas. She received her First Holy Communion when she was eleven. Katharine loved Jesus in the Eucharist for the rest of her life. This prayer is based on her reflections.

You Are the Vine

Jesus in the Holy Eucharist, give yourself to me and to every human heart. You are the vine that in very truth bears God's plants. Send the sap of your divine life into all the branches and shoots, so that we may blossom and bear fruit into eternal life.

St. Katharine Drexel (1858–1955)

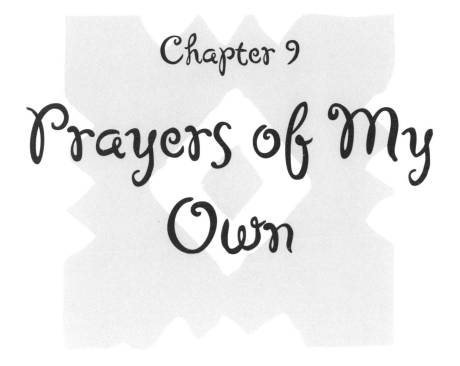

Chapter 9
Prayers of My Own

You can use the following pages to write your own prayers. They can be prayers of thanksgiving, praise, sorrow, asking, or blessing. Just wait to hear the music of God's love in your heart, and then start writing!

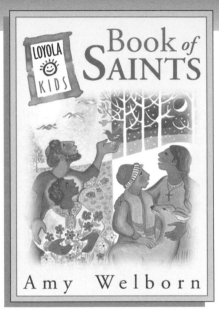